Ghost Hunter's Guide
to
California's
Gold Rush Country

Ghost Hunter's Guide
to
California's
Gold Rush Country

Jeff Dwyer

PELICAN PUBLISHING COMPANY
GRETNA 2009

*The word "Pelican" and the depiction of a pelican
are trademarks of Pelican Publishing Company, Inc.,
and are registered in the U.S. Patent and Trademark Office.*

ISBN-13: 9781589806870

Printed in the United States of America
Published by Pelican Publishing Company, Inc.
1000 Burmaster Street, Gretna, Louisiana 70053

To my daughter,
Sarah Shannon Dwyer

Contents

Acknowledgments

I am deeply indebted to my literary agent, Sue Janet Clark, for her advice, support, and endless patience.

My thanks go to historian Carla Heine who shared with me many ghosts stories from California's early days; to ghost hunters Jackie Ganiy, president of Sonoma SPIRITS, and Sally Aquino, who shared their knowledge and expertise with me; to KFOG producer Greg McQuaid and host Dave Morey for the many opportunities to speak to their radio audience; to the staff of Winchester Mystery House for their interest in my books; and to Darlene, Sam, Michael, and Sarah Dwyer for their support and encouragement.

"Gold! Gold, from the American River."

—Sam Brannan
as he raced through the streets of
San Francisco on March 15, 1848

Introduction

Who believes in ghosts? People from every religion, culture, and generation believe that ghosts exist. The popularity of ghosts and haunted places in books, televisions programs, and movies reflects a belief held by many people that other dimensions and spiritual entities exist.

In 2000, a Gallup poll discovered a significant increase in the number of Americans who believe in ghosts since the question was first asked in 1978. Thirty-one percent of respondents said they believed ghosts existed. In 1978, only 11 percent admitted to believing in ghosts. Less than a year later, Gallup found that 42 percent of the public believed a house could be haunted, but only 28 percent believed that we can hear from or mentally communicate with someone who has died. A 2003 Harris poll found that an astounding 51 percent of Americans believed in ghosts. As with preceding polls, belief in ghosts was greatest among females. More young people accepted the idea of ghosts than older people. Forty-four percent of people aged 18 to 29 years admitted a belief in ghosts compared with 13 percent of those over 65. In 2005, a CBS News poll reported similar findings. Twenty-two percent of the respondents admitted they had personally seen or felt the presence of a ghost. In this same year, Gallup reported that 75 percent of Americans believed in at least one paranormal phenomenon including ESP, reincarnation, spirit channeling, ghosts, and clairvoyance. More recently, in 2007, an Associated Press survey reported that 34 percent of Americans believed in ghosts.

In October 2001, Home and Garden TV conducted a survey on its Web site. When asked, "Do you believe in ghosts?" 87 percent of the respondents said "Yes!" Fifty-one percent indicated they had seen a ghost, but only 38 percent would enter a haunted house alone at night.

Polls and surveys are interesting, but there is no way of knowing how many people have seen or heard a ghost only to feel too embarrassed, foolish, or frightened to admit it. Many ghost hunters and spiritual investigators believe a vast majority of people have seen or heard something from the other world, but failed to recognize it.

Today, a lot of residents and visitors to California's Gold Rush Country believe that ghostly phenomena can be experienced there. This is evidenced by the increased popularity of tours of cemeteries, gold mines, and historic districts in the quaint towns and villages of the region, and the number of paranormal investigations staged by local organizations.

Broadcast and cable television channels recognize the phenomenal nationwide interest in paranormal phenomena. In the summer of 2004, the SciFi channel launched a weekly 1-hour primetime program on ghost hunting. SciFi also airs programs that investigate psychic abilities and many other fascinating topics.

NBC broadcasts a weekly primetime drama called *The Medium* that follows the true-life experiences of a psychic who communicates with ghosts in order to solve crimes. CBS offers another fact-based drama called *Ghost Whisperer* that has become a huge hit. On Friday nights, the Travel Channel presents *Most Haunted* and other ghost documentaries that take viewers all over the world. *A Haunting* on the Discovery Channel presents portrayals of ghostly encounters narrated by the people who had the experience. In December of 2007, the Arts and Entertainment Channel premiered a new series called *Paranormal State* that follows a group of Pennsylvania State University students as they conduct investigations of ghosts and demons.

Internet users will find more than 2.5 million references to ghosts, ghost hunting, haunted places, and related paranormal phenomena. Search engines such as Google can aid ghost hunters in tracking down reports of ghostly activity in almost any city in America, locating paranormal investigative organizations they can join or consult, and purchasing ghost hunting equipment or books that deal with the art and science of finding ghosts.

The recent worldwide interest in ghosts is not a spin-off of the New Age movement, or the current popularity of angels, or the manifestation of some new religious process. The suspicion or recognition that ghosts exist is simply the reemergence of one of mankind's oldest and most basic beliefs: there is a life after death.

Ancient writings from many cultures describe apparitions and a variety of spirit manifestations that include tolling bells, chimes, disembodied crying or moaning, and whispered messages. Legends and ancient books include descriptions of ghosts, dwelling places of spirits, and periods of intense spiritual activity related to seasons or community events such as festivals and crop harvests.

Vital interactions between the living and deceased have been described. Many ancient cultures included dead people or their spirits in community life. Spirits of the dead were sought as a source of guidance, wisdom, and protection for the living. Many followers of the world's oldest religions agree that non-living entities may be contacted for guidance or may be seen on the earthly plane. Among these are visions of saints, the Virgin Mary, and angels.

Ancient sites of intense spiritual activity in Arizona, New Mexico, and Central and South America are popular destinations for travelers seeking psychic or spiritual experiences. More modern, local sites, where a variety of paranormal events have occurred, are also popular destinations for adventurous living souls. Amateur and professional ghost hunters seek the spirits of the dearly departed in the Gold Rush Country's mansions, old theatres, historic bars and inns, firehouses, stores, and countless other places including graveyards and famous hard rock gold mines. Modern buildings, city parks, restaurants and bars, numerous historic sites such as Sutter's mill, and seldom-traveled back country roads also serve as targets for ghost hunters.

Throughout the past two millennia, the popularity of belief in ghosts has waxed and waned, similar to religious activity. When a rediscovery of ghosts and their role in our lives occurs, skeptics label the notion a fad or an aberration of modern lifestyles. Perhaps people are uncomfortable with the idea that ghosts exist because it involves an examination of our nature and our concepts of life, death, and afterlife. These concepts are most often considered in the context of religion, yet ghost hunters recognize that acceptance of the reality of ghosts, and a life after death, is a personal decision, having nothing to do with religious beliefs or church doctrine. An intellectual approach enables the ghost hunter to explore haunted places without religious bias or fear.

The great frequency of ghost manifestations in the Gold Rush region, as evidenced by documentary reports on TV and other news media, reflects some people's open-mindedness and wide-spread interest in ghostly experiences. Ghost hunting is a popular weekend pastime for many adventurous souls. Advertisement of haunted inns, restaurants, and historical sites is commonplace. It is always fun, often very exciting, and may take ghost hunters places they had never dreamed of going.

ABOUT THIS BOOK

Chapter 1 of this book will help you, the ghost hunter, to research and organize your own ghost hunt. Chapters 2 through 6 describe several locations at which ghostly activity has been reported. Unlike other collections of ghost stories and descriptions of haunted places, this book emphasizes access. Addresses of each haunted site are included along with other information to assist you in locating and entering each location. Several appendices offer organizational material for your ghost hunts, including a Sighting Report Form to document your adventures, lists of suggested reading and videos, Internet resources, and organizations you may contact about your experiences with ghosts.

WHAT WAS THE GOLD RUSH?

The rush for gold in California was the greatest event in the history of the American West. When James Marshall discovered gold nuggets in the water way of a lumber mill on January 28, 1848, the discovery set in motion a great migration that brought more than 300,000 gold seekers, merchants, craftsman, farmers, ranchers, land speculators, builders, mining engineers, bandits, and prostitutes to the Sierra foothills. As these people passed through coastal ports, they transformed hamlets and villages into great cities. San Francisco's population grew from less than 1,000 in 1848 to over 25,000 in 1850. The term "forty-niner" is derived from the year in which the greatest migration occurred. In the Sierra foothills, makeshift wooden shanties, barrooms, gambling halls, and stores were built only to be erased by fire months later, in some cases several times. Stalwart residents quickly rebuilt their towns with brick and stone, giving us many fascinating structures that remain today as inns, museums, and restaurants, many of which are inhabited by ghosts.

The great wealth generated by lucky prospectors and large mining operations funded with Eastern capital fostered California's entry into the Union in 1850 and later financed much of the Civil War. By 1862, the Gold Rush was over, but improved mining techniques kept some mines in operation through difficult economic periods. Many California gold mines opened in the 1850s are still in operation today. Prospectors still roam the Sierras, panning in the creeks for gold dust or chipping away at quartz outcroppings for nuggets. It is said that the forty-niners recovered less than ten percent of California's gold.

GHOST HUNTING IN THE GOLD RUSH COUNTRY

The very word *ghost* immediately brings to mind visions of ancient European castles, foggy moors, and dark, wind-swept ramparts where brave knights battled enemies of the crown or heroines threw themselves to their deaths. The fact is that ghosts are everywhere. A history based in antiquity that includes dark dungeons, hidden catacombs, or ancient ruins covered with a veil of sorrow and pain is not essential, but contemporary versions of these elements are common in many American cities.

Indeed, several undeveloped areas of the Sierra foothills and most Gold Rush Country communities have all the ingredients necessary for successful ghost hunting. Indians who inhabited the region for a thousand years or more frequently engaged in intertribal warfare while practicing a spiritual lifestyle that included communication with the dead. Discovery and desecration of their graves during construction of modern roads and buildings have led to reports of spirit activity and disturbing paranormal events.

Since the 1840s, the region has been populated with people from a variety of cultures who experienced tremendous changes in their lives. Changes and challenges that were, at times, over-whelming were created by the transition of the region in 1846 from a wilderness under the tenuous control of Mexico to a nearly lawless American territory. The calamity of the Gold Rush brought thousands of people through coastal and valley cities and over the Sierra Nevada from 1849 to 1858, creating even more turmoil in the region. The growing wealth of cities and towns and the admission of California to the Union in 1850 as the thirty-first state did little to dampen criminal activity, reduce civil disobedience, dissipate racism, or civilize those who abandoned the best qualities of their character while they engaged in the greedy search for gold. Other cataclysmic changes were brought about by armed conflicts, including skirmishes between Indians and white settlers and gold seekers. Examples include the Clear Lake Massacre of 1852, which killed more than 400 Native Americans, the Massacre at the Klamath River in 1854, and the Fresno Massacre of 1854.

One of the earliest skirmishes occurred only six months after gold was discovered. In July of 1848, three advance scouts for a Mormon wagon train were found brutally murdered alongside the Emigrant Trail. The condition of the bodies indicated the men were killed by Indians. Today, the site is called Tragedy Springs and can be reached by Highway 88.

Yellow fever and Cholera epidemics of the 1850s and 1870s brought tragedy to many families, ending lives at a young age and filling many pioneer cemeteries. In many fascinating cemeteries, such as Sacramento's Old City Cemetery, the Pioneer Cemetery of Coloma, and the Old Mormon Tavern Cemetery in Clarksville, many grave markers list specific epidemics as the cause of death. Many also reveal that death came at a young age, creating spirits who have yet to let go and move on.

Catastrophic fires destroyed many Gold Rush country towns and cities in their infancy. These fast-moving blazes destroyed hundreds of wooden shacks and tents, catching many residents off guard and killing them. Among the towns that were turned to ashes and then quickly rebuilt are Grass Valley (1855), Auburn (1850), Murphys (1859, 1874, and 1893), Columbia (1857), Georgetown (1852), Mariposa (1866), Mokelumne Hill (1855, 1865, and 1874), Nevada City (1856 and 1863), Coulterville (1859, 1879, and 1899), and Jamestown (1860 and 1890).

The Jamestown fire of 1890 produced several ghosts that remain active in the Hotel Willow today. Historical accounts of the fire-fighting effort describe desperate and haphazard dynamiting of several buildings in town in an effort to stop the blaze from spreading to the highly-valued Hotel Willow. The dynamiting was done without much coordination, and many people did not hear the warning to evacuate. As a result, several people died when their homes and shops were blown up.

Some of these fires also destroyed wooden grave markers in the town cemeteries. During the period of rapid rebuilding that followed these terrible conflagrations, spirits became restless when buildings were constructed over their unmarked graves. During construction of parks, homes, businesses, and streets, several graves have been opened, leading to reports of ghostly activity in modern structures. Most recently, graves have been discovered during sewer re-construction under the street that passes by Sutter's Fort in Sacramento.

As gold hunters transitioned from panning gravel in streams to digging hard rock tunnels, great wealth was produced but dangers increased. Cave-ins, fires, and flooding of mine shafts occurred with alarming frequency, sometimes closing mines that still held vast amounts of gold. In 1850, a Georgetown mine cave-in killed more than 20 Chinese miners. Rescue was not feasible, so the mine was sealed and the American River Inn built over the spot. In the late 1800s, a mine under the Hotel Willow in Jamestown caved in, trapping 27 miners. No attempt was made to extricate their bodies. These events may account for the much of the ghostly activity experienced by visitors and staff at these businesses. Many bars, inns, and restaurants in Placerville, Sutter Creek, Coulterville, Amador City, and Mokelumne Hill now stand over or near sealed mines or tunnels believed to contain the remains of lost miners.

The most recent large-scale mining tragedy occurred on August 27, 1922, at the Argonaut Gold Mine in Jamestown. An explosion and fire inside the main shaft trapped 47 miners. Rescue attempts captured the attention of the nation, but they were futile, leaving the men entombed under the streets of Jamestown.

The most famous disaster to occur in the Gold Rush country was the Donner party tragedy of 1846. Delayed by Indian attacks, damage to their wagons, desert sands that slowed their pace to two miles per day, and loss of draft animals, the wagon train was caught by early snows in the Sierra Nevada while attempting to cross the rugged mountains on an unproven route. Starving and huddled in their wagons and makeshift shelters for months, 41 men, women, and children suffered a slow, agonizing death. Many of the 46 members who were eventually rescued suffered from frostbite and other illnesses that would shorten their lives. They were also ostracized when stories spread of their cannibalism. The site of this tragedy, now called Donner Lake, is well known for bizarre paranormal experiences.

All of these tragic events add to the region's ghost legacy and have left powerful emotional imprints created by spirits of the dearly departed who felt a need to stay on. A common factor in the creation of a ghost is the loss of life by a sudden, violent event, often at a young age. In the case of the Donner party, some members lingered many days with great emotional anguish and lost hope. Starved, they realized their death was inevitable. This experience may have left their souls with an inextinguishable desire to achieve their life's objectives or with a sense of obligation to offer protection to those who remained alive in their camp.

Some ghosts remain on the earthly plane for revenge or to provide guidance for someone still alive. Many of those who came to California for gold were caught up in their dreams of great wealth but met with only frustration and failure before dying alone and in poverty. Their restless spirits still roam the towns and back roads of Sierra Nevada foothills searching for the elusive yellow metal.

Communities of the Gold Rush country have had their share of criminal activity and social injustice. In Downieville, the story of a Mexican woman named Juanita is still told as an example of ethnic intolerance and cruelty that was commonplace in most Gold Rush towns in the 1850s. Accused of murder, a swift trial conducted by a judge and jury composed of white gold miners produced a guilty verdict and death sentence. Juanita was hung from the Yuba River Bridge, where her ghost still walks. Several other mining towns were known for swift justice at the end of a rope. So many lynchings were carried out in Placerville that the place became known as Hangtown, a town nickname still widely recognized throughout Northern California today. In some areas, mob justice and a prominent hanging tree in the center of town had a sobering effect on outlaws. Some hangings, though, had intense overtones of racism. In a barn on the Stevenot Winery property in Murphys, an Indian was hung without the accusation of a crime.

In 1860 at Chinese Camp, on Highway 49 south of Jamestown, a "tong" war broke out among four of six large protective associations. Fostered by large tong in San Francisco, these associations were based on ancestral and social factors that included region of origin in China. With a population of 5,000 in the mid-1850s, tong rivalry reached its peak, culminating in a local war that decimated the weaker tongs. Today, little remains of Chinese Camp, but sensitive people will find some active spirits there.

Famous outlaws, such as stage coach robber Black Bart and horse thief Joaquin Murrieta, have left their mark on the Gold Rush country. Black Bart's ghost has been spotted at several locations including the Murphys Hotel, a back road near Copperopolis, the Wells Fargo office in Columbia, and the Swiss Hotel in Sonoma, where legend says he was shot to death. The ghost of Joaquin Murrieta has also been seen in Murphys where, it is said, his crime spree started in 1850. Before his death in 1853, he supposedly killed more than three hundred men and amassed a treasure of stolen goods that has never been found. Joaquin was such a feared predator that his head was cut off by Captain Harry Love's posse and displayed in a glass jar throughout the Gold Rush country for many years. The hand of Murrieta's companion, Three-fingered Jack, was also displayed to dispel the fears of law-abiding society. These historical artifacts were lost in the fire that consumed much of San Francisco after the 1906 earthquake.

Lesser known outlaws have also left their mark, and their ghosts, in the Gold Rush country. In 1854, Tom Bell escaped from Angel Island Prison, on San Francisco Bay, formed a gang with five other desperados, and robbed stages for several months before they were captured. Bell was hung by a vigilante mob in Nevada City on October 4, 1856. Others with colorful names–Rattlesnake Dick, Monte Jack, English Bob, and Holden Dick–have left behind graves, cabins, jails, hanging trees, saloons, and hotels where they gambled, fought, pondered their miserable lives, and died. In many of these places, the ghosts of these Gold Rush outlaws can still be found.

The heinous crimes of modern criminals have also produced ghosts by cutting short the lives of people who still had goals, dreams, obligations, or loved ones to care for. In Sacramento, the grounds surrounding the home of Dorothea Puente have been investigated by local ghost hunters, who have obtained some interesting EVP. From 1982 to 1988, Puente took in elderly boarders then killed them so she could support herself with their social security checks. She buried nine of her victims in her backyard, then planted a vegetable garden over the site. In the 1980s, Leonard Lake and Charles Ng kidnapped several people, held them in cages on a remote property near Wilseyville, and subjected them to torture and extreme abuse. Some of their heinous crimes were recorded on video tape. The two were eventually convicted of 11 murders. Remains of many of their victims have never been found. The prospect of lost spirits has intrigued local ghost hunters, but residents of the area are not eager to share their knowledge of the crime scenes.

The activities of these outlaws produced many used, abused, confused, and forlorn spirits who remain with us after their deaths. The spirits of these victims may still seek lost dreams while they remain attached to what little they gained during their difficult lives. Many ghosts who harbor deep resentment, pain, or a desire to complete their unfinished business still roam the darkened halls of court houses, hotels, theatres, cemeteries, modern buildings, and many other places throughout the region that are accessible to the public.

WHAT IS A GHOST?

A ghost is some aspect of the personality, spirit, consciousness, energy, mind, or soul that remains after the body dies. When any of these are detected by the living–through sight, sound, odor, or movement– the manifestation is called an apparition by parapsychologists. The rest of us call it a ghost. How the ghost manifests itself is unknown. There seems to be a close association, however, between aspects of the entity's life and whether it manifests itself as a ghost. These include a sudden, traumatic death; strong ties to a particular place or loved ones who survived the entity; unfinished business; strong emotions such as hatred and anger, or a desire for revenge.

Ghosts differ from other paranormal phenomena by their display of intelligent action. This includes interaction with the living, performance of a purposeful activity, or a response to on-going changes in the environment. Ghosts may speak to the living to warn of an unforeseen accident or disaster, to give advice, or to express their love, anger, remorse, or disappointment. They may also be trying to complete some project or duty they failed to finish before death. Some ghosts try to move furniture, room decorations or the like, to suit their preferences.

Some ghosts appear solid and function as living beings because they are unaware they are dead. Others appear as partial apparitions because they are confused about their transition from life to death.

Occasionally, paranormal activity is bizarre, frightening or dangerous. Witnesses may see objects fly about, hear strange sounds, or experience accidents. This kind of activity is attributed to a "poltergeist" or noisy ghost. Most authorities believe that a living person, not the dead, causes these manifestations. Generally, someone under great emotional stress releases psychic energy that creates subtle or spectacular changes in the environment.

Noises commonly associated with a poltergeist include tapping on walls or ceilings, heavy footsteps, shattered glass, ringing telephones, and running water. Objects may move about on tables or floors or fly across a room. Furniture may spin or tip over. Dangerous objects, such as knives, hammers, or pens, may hit people. These poltergeist events may last a few days, a year, or more. Discovery and removal of the emotionally unstable, living person often stops the poltergeist.

HAUNTINGS

Hauntings and ghost apparitions appear to be similar, but they are not the same thing. Many professional ghost hunters and parapsychologists are careful to make a clear distinction between these two kinds of paranormal phenomena. They share a lot of the same features in terms of what witnesses see, feel, or smell, but a haunting may occur without the presence of a spiritual entity or the consciousness of a dead person. People have reported seeing pale, transparent images of the deceased walking in hallways, climbing stairs, sitting in rocking chairs, or sitting on airplanes, trains, buses, and even in restaurants. Some have been seen sleeping in beds, hanging by a rope from a tree, or walking through walls. Most commonly, a partial apparition is seen, but witnesses have reported seeing entire armies engaged in battle. Unlike ghosts, hauntings do not display intelligent action with respect to their location–they do not manipulate your new computer–and they do not interact with the living.

Hauntings may be environmental imprints or recordings of something that happened at a specific location as a result of the repetition of intense emotion. As such, they tend to be associated with a specific place or object, not a particular person. The ghostly figures tend to perform some kind of repetitive task or activity. Sometimes the haunting is so repetitive that witnesses feel as though they are watching a video loop that plays the same brief scene over and over. A good example is the image of a deceased grandmother who makes appearances seated in her favorite rocking chair.

There is a lot of evidence that people can trigger and experience these environmental recordings by visiting the particular site, touching an object that was a key element of the event, and psychically connecting with the event. Images of hauntings have been recorded digitally and on still and video film. The location of strong environmental imprints can also be discovered through devices such as electromagnetic field detectors. Higher magnetic readings have been found at locations where psychics frequently experience hauntings.

HOW DOES A GHOST MANIFEST ITSELF?

Ghosts interact with our environment in a variety of ways that may have something to do with the strength of their personality or the level of confusion concerning their transformation by death. The talents or skills they possessed in life, their personal objectives, or their level of frustration may be their reason for trying to get our attention. Some ghosts create odors or sounds, particularly those associated with their habits, such as cigar smoke or whistling. Many reports mention the odors of tobacco, oranges, and hemp as most common. Sounds, including voice messages, may be detected with an audio recorder (see Electronic Voice Phenomenon). Ghost hunters have recorded greetings, warnings, screams, sobbing, and expressions of love.

One of the most common ghostly activities is moving objects. Ghosts like to knock over stacks of cards or coins, turn doorknobs, scatter matchsticks, and move your keys. For many it appears easy to manipulate light switches and TV remotes, open and close windows and doors, or push chairs around. Some ghosts have the power to throw objects, pull pictures from walls, or move heavy items. As a rule, ghosts cannot tolerate disturbances within the place they haunt. If you tilt a wall-mounted picture, the ghost will set it straight. Obstacles placed in the ghost's path may be pushed aside.

These seemingly minor indications of ghostly activity should be recorded for future reference on the Sighting Report Form in Appendix A.

Ghosts can also create changes in the physical qualities of an environment. Ice-cold breezes and unexplained gusts of wind are often the first signs that a ghost is present. Moving or stationary cold spots, with temperatures several degrees below surrounding areas, have been detected with reliable instruments. Temperature changes sometimes occur with a feeling that the atmosphere has thickened as if the room was suddenly filled with unseen people.

In searching for ghosts, some people use devices that detect changes in magnetic, electrical, or radio fields. However, detected changes may be subject to error, interference by other electrical devices, or misinterpretation. Measurements indicating the presence of a ghost may be difficult to capture on a permanent record.

Ghosts may create images on still cameras (film or digital) and video recorders such as luminous fogs, balls of light called orbs, streaks of light, or the partial outline of body parts. In the 1860s, this was called "spirit photography." Modern digital photographs are easily edited and make it difficult to produce convincing proof of ghostly activity.

Humanoid images are the prized objective of most ghost hunters, but they are also the least produced. When such images occur, they are often partial, revealing only a head and torso with an arm or two. Feet are seldom seen. Full body apparitions are extremely rare. Some ghost hunters have seen ethereal, fully transparent forms that are barely discernible. Others report seeing ghosts who appear as solid as a living being.

WHY DO GHOSTS REMAIN AT A PARTICULAR PLACE?

Ghosts remain in a particular place because they are emotionally attached to a room, a building, or special surroundings that profoundly affected them during their lives, or to activities or events that played a role in their death. A prime example is the haunted house inhabited by the ghost of a man who hung himself in the master bedroom because his wife left him. It is widely believed that death and sudden transition from the physical world confuse a ghost. He or she remains in familiar or emotionally stabilizing surroundings to ease the strain. A place-bound ghost is most likely to occur when a violent death occurred with great emotional anguish. Ghosts may linger in a house, barn, cemetery, factory, or store waiting for a loved one or anyone familiar that might help them deal with their new level of existence. Some ghosts wander through buildings or forests, on bridges, or alongside particular sections of roads. Some await enemies, seeking revenge. Others await a friend for a chance to resolve their guilt.

UNDER WHAT CONDITIONS IS A SIGHTING MOST LIKELY?

Although ghosts may appear at any time, a sighting may occur on special holidays, anniversaries, birthdays, or during historic periods (for example, July 4 or December 7) or calendar periods pertaining to the personal history of the ghost. Halloween is reputed to be a favorite night for many apparitions, while others seem to prefer their own special day or night, on a weekly or monthly cycle.

Night is a traditional time for ghost activity, yet experienced ghost hunters know that sightings may occur at any time. There seems to be no consistent affinity of ghosts for darkness, but they seldom appear when artificial light is bright. Perhaps this is why ghosts shy away from camera crews and their array of lights. Ghosts seem to prefer peace and quiet, although some of them have been reported to make incessant, loud sounds. Even a small group of ghost hunters may make too much noise to facilitate a sighting. For this reason, it is recommended that you limit your group to four persons and oral communication be kept to a minimum.

IS GHOST HUNTING DANGEROUS?

Ghost hunting can be hazardous, but reports of injuries inflicted by ghosts are rare and their veracity suspect. Movies and children's ghost stories have created a widespread notion that ghosts may harm the living or even cause the death of persons they dislike. In 2006, a popular television program showed a fascinating video of a ghost hunter being struck down by his camera equipment. The man's heavy equipment moved suddenly from a position at his waist and struck him on the side of the face. Video of this event was interpreted as evidence of a ghost attack, but no apparition or light anomaly was visible. Decades ago, the Abbot of Trondheim ghost was reputed to have attacked some people, but circumstances and precipitating events are unclear.

Many authorities believe that rare attacks by ghosts are a matter of mistaken identity, i.e., the ghost misidentified a living person as a figure the ghost knew during his life. It is possible that encounters that appear to be attacks may be nothing more than clumsy efforts by a ghost to achieve recognition. Witnesses of ghost appearances have found themselves in the middle of gunfights, major military battles, and other violent events, yet sustained not the slightest injury.

Persons who claim to have been injured by a ghost have, in most cases, precipitated the injury themselves through their own ignorance or fear. Ghost hunters often carry out investigations in the dark or subdued light and may encounter environmental hazards that lead to injury. Fear may trigger an attempt to race from a haunted site, exposing the ghost hunter to injury by tripping over unseen objects or making contact with broken glass, low-hanging tree limbs, exposed wiring, or weakened floorboards, stairways, or doorways.

The ghost hunter will be safe if he keeps a wary eye and calm attitude and sets aside tendencies to fear the ghost or the circumstances of its appearance. Safety may be enhanced if you visit a haunted location while it is well illuminated, during daylight hours for instance. Potential hazards in the environment can be identified and, perhaps, cleared or marked with light-reflecting tape.

Most authorities agree that ghosts do not travel. Ghosts will not follow you home, take up residence in your car, or attempt to occupy your body. They are held in time and space by deep emotional ties to an event or place. Ghosts have been observed on airplanes, trains, buses, and ships: however, it is unlikely that the destination interests them. Something about the journey, some event such as a plane crash or train wreck, accounts for their appearance as travelers. It some cases, it is the conveyance that ties the ghost to the physical plane. A vintage World War II B-17 bomber may be haunted by the ghost of a man who piloted that type of aircraft in the 1940s. A ship, such as the *Queen Mary* in Long Beach, CA, may be an irresistible attraction for the ghost of a sailor who once worked on passenger liners.

HOT SPOTS FOR GHOSTLY ACTIVITY

Numerous sites of disasters, criminal activity, suicides, devastating fires, and other tragic events abound in California's Gold Rush country, providing hundreds of opportunities for ghost hunting. You may visit the locations described in Chapters 2-6 to experience ghostly activity discovered by others, or discover a hot spot to research and initiate your own ghost investigation.

Astute ghost hunters often search historical maps, drawings, and other documents to find the sites of military conflicts, buildings that no longer exist, or sites of tragic events now occupied by modern structures. For example, maps and drawings found online or displayed in museums such as the Discovery Museum Gold Rush History Center in Sacramento, the El Dorado County Historical Museum in Placerville, or historic locations such as Gold Discovery Park in Coloma may be a good place to start.

People who died in mine disasters or train or stagecoach robberies, of epidemics or infections that ensued after minor injuries, who succumbed to the hard life of an unsuccessful gold prospector, and those displaced by other tragic events such as fires, may haunt the site of their graves, favorite bars or restaurants, workplaces, or cherished homes.

In some of Sacramento's older neighborhoods, homes of many well-known residents, such as railroad magnate Leland Stanford who later founded Stanford University in Palo Alto, and the old Governor's Mansion, built in 1877, are reputed to harbor ghosts. Fascinating histories and ghostly atmospheres may be found in historic homes such as the Red Castle in Nevada City, the Bourn Mansion at the Empire Mine near Nevada City, the Lola Montez house in Grass Valley, the Vineyard House and Thomas Hanford Williams house in Coloma, the Combellack-Blair House in Placerville, the Bernhard House in Auburn, and the John J. Snyder House and Wyllie House in San Andreas. Many of these historic buildings are popular weekend destinations for ghost hunters. Access is easy since many of these places are bed-and-breakfast inns, restaurants and bars, museums, or shops.

Some towns have established historic districts and other venues that have been investigated by professional and amateur ghost hunters. These include the preserved and restored gold rush town of Columbia, the historic West Main Street of Nevada City, the Old Town section of Auburn, the Gold Discovery State Park in Coloma, the Empire Mine near Grass Valley, and Old Sacramento.

Many churches dating from the mid-nineteenth century exist throughout the Gold Rush country, including the gateway cities of Sacramento, Folsom, and Stockton. Some of these old places of worship include a graveyard. Most of them, such as the 1859-vintage St. James Episcopal Church in Sonora, the 1851 Methodist Episcopal Church in Placerville, and the St. Francis Xavier Catholic Church in Chinese Camp, are restored and accessible to visitors as points of historical interest. Other historic places of worship, such as Trinity Episcopal Church in Nevada City (1873), St. James Anglican Church in Sonora (1860), the Jamestown Community Methodist Church (1852), and the Methodist Church in Auburn (1858) still offer worship services. The grounds of some of these fascinating places contain graves of well-known pioneers, in addition to mass graves of those who died in mining disasters and the epidemics of the nineteenth century. Mount Saint Mary's Convent and Academy in Grass Valley will also interest ghost hunters.

Several cemeteries dating from the mid-nineteenth century are scattered about the region and known by local ghost hunters as good places to experience paranormal phenomena. Many of them have fascinating architecture, epitaphs, and lists of occupants, in addition to a spooky atmosphere. These cities of the dead include some unusual tombs and crypts, some marked by peculiar monuments.

The Pioneer Cemetery on Cold Springs Road in Coloma, near the gold discovery site, was opened in 1849 to serve a wild and thriving community of miners, saloon owners, shopkeepers, and prostitutes. Hundreds of people have reported seeing a lady dressed in a burgundy-colored gown standing at the side of the road beckoning passersby to enter the cemetery. Other spirits in this spooky cemetery create orbs in photographs and digital images or create cold spots and that creepy feeling that you are being watched or touched by invisible hands.

In Calaveras County, near San Andreas, a cemetery houses the remains of locals who served as Union soldiers, sailors, and marines during the Civil War. Other fascinating cemeteries containing graves of Gold Rush-era pioneers can be found in Nevada City, Grass Valley, Rough and Ready, Amador City, Colombia, Coloma, Jamestown, and Georgetown.

In Mokelumne Hill, the Protestant Cemetery contains the remains of Louise Leger (1834-1861), wife of local hotel builder George Leger. The ghostly sound of sobbing that has been detected at this gravesite may be a spirit remnant of George, who was murdered in 1879. My great-grandfather is buried in Foresthill Community Cemetery. He died while carrying mail, on snowshoes, between mines in the Sierra Nevada. There are so many spirits in this cemetery it is difficult to focus on one long enough to gain information about the ghost's history.

In the gateway city of Folsom, two cemeteries are well-known for EVP. Lakeside Cemetery and St. John the Baptist Catholic Cemetery both contain the remains of Gold Rush pioneers in addition to Civil War veterans. The old City Cemetery in Sacramento contains more than twenty thousand graves, including those of luminaries such as John A. Sutter, Jr., hotel magnate Marks Hopkins, railroad developer Edwin Crocker, and William Hamilton, son of Alexander Hamilton. Here you will also find the graves of other fascinating people, such as grave robber George D. Gardiner; Manuel Nevis, who died by drowning in a vat of wine; John J. Gray, who committed suicide in 1889 while standing at the side of his daughter's grave; and the singer, Maria Rupp, who was murdered in 1857 by Peter Metz.

Most county websites list pioneer cemeteries and offer links to local organizations that care for the graves and grounds.The best way to see the cemeteries of the Gold Rush country, and learn fascinating histories of those entombed is to tour them with a knowledgeable guide. (See Appendix F: Tours and Events.) These places are too spooky and possibly unsafe after dark unless you are accompanied by people who can ensure a pleasant visit.

LOCAL GHOST HUNTERS

Three local organizations dedicated to ghost hunting are active in the Northern California region. They can help you locate haunted sites, provide information about previous ghost investigations they have conducted, or sharpen your skills as a paranormal investigator. These organizations include Haunted and Paranormal Investigations (HPI), Ghost Trackers, and the San Joaquin Valley Paranormal Investigators (SJVPI). The activities of these organizations have been featured in a variety of news media. Their investigators combine advanced high-tech approaches to ghost hunting with the insight of psychics to produce some amazing results. HPI and Ghost Trackers also host special events and offers classes and training seminars. See Appendix E (Internet Resources) for contact information. Tours of haunted places are available in Nevada City and Colombia (see Appendix F). If you inquire at a local bookshop or historical society, you may meet a history buff or ghost hunter who can take you places tourists rarely hear about.

TWO SIMPLE RULES

Two simple rules apply for successful ghost hunting. The first is to be patient. Ghosts are everywhere, but contact may require a considerable investment of time. The second rule is to have fun.

You may report your ghost hunting experiences or suggest hot spots for ghost hunting to the author via e-mail at **Ghosthunter@jeffdwyer. com.** Visit the author's Web site at **www.jeffdwyer.com.**

Ghost Hunter's Guide
to
California's
Gold Rush Country

CHAPTER 1

How to Hunt for Ghosts

You may want to visit recognized haunted sites, listed in Chapters 2 through 6, using some of the ghost hunting techniques described later in this chapter. Or, you may want to conduct your own spirit investigation. If that is the case, choose a place you think might be haunted, like an old house in your neighborhood or a favorite bed-and-breakfast inn. You may get a lead from fascinating stories about ancestors that have been passed down through your family.

Your search for a ghost or exploration of a haunted place starts with research. Summaries of obscure and esoteric material about possible haunted sites are available from museums, local historical societies, and bookstores. Brochures and booklets, sold at historical sites under the California State Park system, can be good resources, too.

Guided tours of historical sites, such as the preserved 19th century town of Columbia; old neighborhoods in towns such as Nevada City, Grass Valley, and Sonora; historic Main Street in Placerville; or old churches, mines, and pioneer cemeteries throughout the Gold Rush country, are good places to begin your research. Tours can help you develop a feel for places within a building where ghosts might be sighted or an appreciation of relevant history. Gold Rush country ghost, cemetery, and history tours are very popular and offer a good way to learn a lot about local paranormal activity in a short time.

By touring haunted buildings, you will have opportunities to speak with guides and docents who may be able to provide you with clues about the dearly departed or tell you ghost stories you can't find in published material. Docents may know people—old-timers in the area or amateur historians—who can give you additional information about a site, its former owners or residents, and its potential for ghostly activity.

Almost every city has a local historical society (see Appendix G). These are good places to find information that may not be published anywhere else. This could be histories of local families and buildings; information about tragedies, disasters, criminal activity, or legends; and myths about places that may be haunted. You will want to take notes about secret scandals or other ghost-producing happenings that occurred at locations now occupied by modern buildings, roads, or parks. In these cases, someone occupying a new house or other structure could hear strange sounds, feel cold spots, or see ghosts or spirit remnants.

Newspapers are an excellent source of historical information, as well. You can search for articles about ghosts, haunted places, or paranormal activity by accessing the newspaper's archives via the Internet and entering key words, dates, or names. Newspaper articles about suicides, murders, train wrecks, plane crashes, and paranormal phenomena can often provide essential information for your ghost hunt. Stories about authentic haunted sites are common around Halloween.

Bookstores and libraries usually have special-interest sections with books on local history by local writers. A few inquiries may connect you with these local writers who may be able to help you focus your research.

If these living souls cannot help, try the dead. A visit to a local graveyard is always fruitful in identifying possible ghosts. Often you can find headstones that indicate the person entombed died of suicide, criminal activity, local disaster, or such. Some epitaphs may indicate if the deceased was survived by a spouse and children or died far from home.

Perhaps the best place to start a search for a ghost is within your own family. Oral histories can spark your interest in a particular ancestor, scandal, building, or site relevant to your family. Old photographs, death certificates, letters and wills, anniversary lists in family Bibles, and keepsakes can be great clues. Then you can visit gravesites or homes of your ancestors to check out the vibes as you mentally and emotionally empathize with specific aspects of your family's history.

Almost every family has a departed member who died at an early age, suffered hardships or emotional anguish, or passed away suddenly due to an accident or natural disaster. Once you have focused your research on a deceased person, you need to determine if that person remains on this earthly plane as a ghost. Evaluate the individual's personal history to see if he had a reason to remain attached to a specific place.

Was his death violent or under tragic circumstances?

Did he die at a young age with unfinished business?

Did the deceased leave behind loved ones who needed his support and protection?

Was this person attached to a specific site or building?

Would the individual be inclined to seek revenge against those responsible for his death?

Would his devotion and sense of loyalty lead him to offer eternal companionship to loved ones?

Revenge, anger, refusal to recognize the reality of transformation by death, and other negative factors prompt many spirits to haunt places and people. However, most ghosts are motivated by positive factors. Spirits may remain at a site to offer protection to a loved one or a particular place.

Also, remember that ghosts can appear as animals or objects. Apparitions of ships, buildings, covered wagons, bridges, and roads by the strictest definitions are phantoms. A phantom is the essence of a structure that no longer exists on the physical plane. Many people have seen houses, cottages, castles, villages, and large ships that were destroyed or sunk years before.

BASIC PREPARATION FOR GHOST HUNTING

If you decide to ghost hunt at night or on a special anniversary, make a trip to the site a few days ahead of time. During daylight hours, familiarize yourself with the place and its surroundings. Many historical sites are closed after sunset or crowded at certain times by organized tours.

TWO BASIC METHODS FOR FINDING GHOSTS

Based partly on the kind of paranormal activity reported at a site, the ghost hunter must decide which method or approach will be used. Some will feel competent with a collection of cameras, electromagnetic field detectors, digital thermometers, computers, data recorders, and other high-tech gadgets. These ghost hunters prefer to use the Technical Approach. Others may discover they have an emotional affinity for a particular historic site, a surprising fascination with an event associated with a haunting, or empathy for a deceased person. These ghost hunters may have success with the Psychic Approach. Another consideration is the ghost hunter's goal. Some desire scientific evidence of a ghost while others simply want to experience paranormal activity.

THE TECHNICAL APPROACH

Professional ghost hunters often use an array of detection and recording devices that cover a wide range of the electromagnetic spectrum. This approach can be complicated, expensive, and require technically skilled people to operate the devices. Amateur ghost hunters can get satisfying results with simple audio and video recording devices.

Equipment Preparation

A few days before your ghost hunt purchase fresh film for your camera and tape for audio recording devices. Test your batteries and bring backup batteries and power packs with you. You should have two types of flashlights: a broad-beam light for moving around a site and a penlight-type flashlight for narrow-field illumination while you make notes or adjust equipment. A candle is a good way to light the site in a way that is least offensive to a ghost.

Still-Photography Techniques

Many photographic techniques that work well under normal conditions are inadequate for ghost hunts. That's because ghost hunting is usually conducted under conditions of low ambient light. This requires the use of long exposures. Some investigators use a strobe or flash device but these can make the photos look unauthentic or create artifacts, generating the appearance of something that is not truly present.

If you use film-based photography, practice taking photos with films of various light sensitivities before you go on your ghost hunt. Standard photographic films of high light sensitivity should be used—ASA of 800 or higher is recommended. At a dark or nearly dark location, mount the camera on a tripod. Try several exposure settings, from one to 30 seconds, and aperture settings under various low-light conditions.

Make notes about the camera settings that work best under various light conditions. Avoid aiming the camera at a scene where there is a bright light such as a street lamp or exit sign over a doorway. These light sources may "overflow" throughout your photograph.

Some professional ghost hunters use infrared film. You should consult a professional photo lab technician about this type of film and its associated photographic techniques. Amateur ghost hunters have used Polaroid-type cameras with interesting results. The rapid film developing system used by these cameras gives almost instant feedback about your technique and/or success in documenting ghost activities. Ghosts have reportedly written messages on Polaroid film.

If you plan to use digital photographic methods, practice taking pictures under conditions of low ambient light, with and without artificial lighting. Most digital cameras have default automatic settings that might not work well during a ghost hunt. These settings may not be easily changed as ambient conditions change unless you have practiced the procedures. Many of these cameras have features that enable automatic exposures at specific intervals, e.g., once every minute. This allows a hands-off remote photograph record to be made. Repetitive automatic exposures also allow a site to be investigated without the presence of the investigator.

Your equipment should include a stable, lightweight tripod. Hand-held cameras may produce poorly focused photographs when the exposure duration is greater that $\frac{1}{60}$ second.

Audio Recording Techniques

Tape recorders provide an inexpensive way to obtain evidence of ghostly activity, particularly electronic voice phenomena or EVP. A recording mechanism is necessary because the human ear cannot detect EVP directly, as they do not generate sound waves, which vibrate the eardrum. Always test your recorder under conditions you expect to find at the investigation site in order to reduce audio artifact and ensure optimal performance of the device.

Does your recorder pick up excessive background noise? This may obscure ghostly sounds. If so, consider upgrading the tape quality or select a digital audio recorder. Also, consider using a wind guard on the microphone.

Use two or more recorders at different locations within the site. This allows you to verify sounds such as wind against a window and reduce the possibility of ambiguous recordings.

You can use sound-activated recorders at a site overnight. They will automatically switch on whenever a sound occurs above a minimum threshold. Be aware that each sound on the tape may start with an annoying artifact, the result of a slow tape speed at the beginning of each recorded segment. The slow tape speed could obscure the sounds made by a ghost.

Remote microphones and monitor earphones allow you to remain some distance from the site and activate the recorder when ghostly sounds are heard. If this equipment is not available, use long-play modes (60-90 minutes), turn the recorder on, and let it run throughout your hunt, whether you remain stationary or walk about the site. This will provide you with a means of making audio notes rather than written notes. A headset with a microphone is especially useful with this technique.

Ghost hunters who use audio equipment usually seek electronic voice phenomena, EVP. The American Association for EVP defines the process as any intelligible voices detected on recording medium that has no known explanation. EVP may also include the sound of moving objects, such as doors, windows, glass objects, whistling, sobbing, laughter, humming, gun shots, footsteps, musical notes, or knocking.

EVP are captured by one of two ways. They may be encoded on the magnetic tape or electronics of the recording device by manipulation of the local electro-magnetic field or recorder electronics by the spirit. Or, a vocalization, musical note, or other sound that was previously imprinted on the electro-magnetic field of the environment may be triggered by the ghost hunter and detected by the recording device.

Ghost hunters must carefully analyze their audio recordings, and the environment in which they are obtained, to be certain they are not inadvertent recordings of natural or normal sounds. Sound may carry great distances, particularly when there is fog or low overcast. Using a new tape may reduce the chances of artifact.

EVP may be recorded while the ghost hunter remains stationary at a site, such as next to a grave, or while walking around a location. This is called an EVP sweep. Generally, questions are asked to which spirits may respond. These questions should be brief and simple and follow an invitation for any spirits present to communicate. Allow time, from

15 to 60 seconds, for a response. If you know the history of the ghost you seek, your questions can be specific, such as, "Did you die in this bathroom?" or "Did you hang yourself from these rafters?"

EVP can be heard only during playback, so ghost hunters should review recordings every three to five minutes during the interview rather than waiting until their investigation is completed. This will enable the identification of hot spots for spirit activity that should be investigated most thoroughly. The American Association for EVP maintains a Web site for general information and advice: www. AA-EVP.com. Several websites may be accessed to hear examples of EVP. Use a search engine aimed at "EVP" to locate them.

Video Recording

Video recorders offer a wide variety of recording features from time-lapse to auto-start/stop and auto-focus. These features enable you to make surveillance-type recordings over many hours while you are off-site. Consult your user's manual for low-light recording guidelines and always use a tripod and long-duration battery packs.

If you plan to attempt video recording, consider using two recorders, at equal distance from a specific object such as a chair. Arrange the recorders at different angles, preferably 90 degrees from each other.

Another approach you might try is to use a wide-angle setting on the first camera get a broad view of a room, porch, or courtyard. On the second camera, use a close-up setting to capture ghostly apparitions at a door, chair, or window.

You may have more success with sequential, manual, or timer-actuated tape runs than a continuous-record technique. If you try this technique, use tape runs of one to five minutes. Practice using the method that interrupts the automatic setting should you need to manually control the recording process. Always use a tripod that can be moved to a new location in a hurry.

High-Tech Equipment

Night vision goggles can be useful in low-light situations. You can see doors and other objects move that you might not otherwise see. These goggles are quite expensive, however.

You can buy devices such as electromagnetic field detectors, infrared thermometers, barometers, and motion detectors at your local electronics store or over the Internet. A good source for high-tech ghost hunting equipment is www.technica.com. Electronic gadgets can be useful and fun, but unless you have a means of recording the output your reports of anomalies, movement, and apparitions will not be the kind of hard evidence you need to satisfy skeptics.

Other Equipment

Various authorities in the field of ghost hunting suggest the following items to help you mark sites, detect paranormal phenomena, and collect evidence of ghostly activity.

> White and colored chalk
> Compass
> Stop watch
> Steel tape measure
> Magnifying glass
> First aid kit
> Thermometer
> Metal detector
> Graph paper for diagrams
> Small mirror
> Small bell
> Plastic bags for collecting evidence
> Matches
> Tape for sealing doors
> String
> A Cross
> A Bible
> Cell phone

THE PSYCHIC APPROACH

The Psychic Approach relies upon your intuition, inner vision, or emotional connection with a deceased person, object, place, or point of time in history. You don't have to be a trained psychic to use this approach. All of us have some capacity to tap into unseen dimensions.

People who feel the peculiar atmosphere of a distant time or who believe they can perceive a voice, sound, image, touch, or texture of another dimension may have psychic abilities that will payoff in a ghost hunt. The Psychic Approach does require an ability to eliminate external and internal distractions and focus your perceptions. If you use this approach, three factors may increase your chances of experiencing ghostly activity.

The first factor is the strength of the emotional imprint or attachment of the deceased for a particular place. The frequency, duration, and consistency of the paranormal events may indicate the strength of the imprint. The strongest imprints are created by intense emotions such as fear, rage, jealously, revenge, or loss, especially if they were repetitive over long periods of time prior to death. Other emotions such as love for a person, a place, or an object may also create a strong imprint. Biographical research may reveal this kind of information, particularly if personal letters or diaries are examined. Old newspaper articles and photographs are useful, too.

The second factor is the degree of sensitivity the investigator has for a spiritual presence or an environmental imprint. Knowledge of the key elements and historical context of the entity's death can increase your sensitivity. This includes architectural elements of a home, theatre, airplane or ship, furniture, clothing, weapons, or any implement or artifact of the specific time period. Touching or handling these artifacts, or standing within the historic site, enables ghost hunters to get in touch with the historical moment of the ghost's imprint. A high degree of sensitivity for a past era often generates an odd feeling of being transported through time.

The third factor is sensitivity to or empathy for the ghost's lingering presence at a haunted site. A ghost may be trapped, confused, or have chosen to remain at a site to protect someone or guard something precious. Sensitivity for the ghost's predicament can be increased through knowledge of the entity's personal history, such as emotions, motivations, problems, or unfinished business at the time of death. Researching historical sources like newspapers, old photographs, or books can provide this kind of information. Useful, intimate details might be found in letters, suicide notes, diaries, and wills.

Your sensitivity to ghostly environmental imprints and spirit manifestations may be increased by meditation. This is a simple process of relaxing one's physical body to eliminate distracting thoughts and tensions and achieve emotional focus.

Meditation allows you to focus your spiritual awareness on a single subject—a place, entity, or historic moment in time. As the subject comes into focus, you can add information obtained from your research. Markers of time or seasons, artifacts or implements, furniture and doorways are a few suggestions. By doing this, you become aware of unseen dimensions of the world around you that create a feeling that you have moved through time to a distant era. This process gets you in touch with the place, date, and time pertinent to a ghost's imprint or death. The process also enables you to disregard personal concerns and distracting thoughts that may interfere with your concentration on the ghost you seek.

Keep in mind that it is possible to be in a meditative state while appearing quite normal. The process is simple and easy to learn. When you arrive at the site of your ghost hunt, find a place a short distance away to meditate. Three essentials for any effective meditation are comfort, quiet, and concentration.

Comfort: Sit or stand in a relaxed position. Take free and even breaths at a slow rate. Do not alter your breathing pattern so much that you feel short of breath, winded, or lightheaded. Close your eyes if that enhances your comfort, or focus on a candle, tree, or flower. Do not fall asleep. Proper meditation creates relaxation without decreasing alertness.

Quiet: Meditate in a place away from noises generated by traffic, passersby, radios, slammed doors, and the like. If you are with a group, give each other sufficient personal space. Some people use mantras, repetitive words or phrases, or speak only in their mind in order to facilitate inner calmness. Mantras are useful to induce a focused state of relaxation, but they may disrupt the meditation of a companion if spoken aloud. A majority of ghost hunters do not believe that mantras are necessary in this instance. They point out that ghost hunting is not like a séance as depicted in old movies. It is not necessary to chant special words, call out to the dead, or invite an appearance "from beyond the grave."

Concentration: First, clear your mind of everyday thoughts, worries, and concerns. This is the most difficult part of the process. Many of us don't want to let go of our stressful thoughts. To help you let go of those thoughts, let the thought turn off its light and fade into darkness. After you clear your mind, some thoughts may reappear. Repeat the process. Slowly turn off the light of each thought until you can rest with a completely cleared mind. This might take some practice. Don't wait until you are on the scene of a ghost hunt before you practice this exercise.

Once your mind is clear, focus on your breathing, and imagine your entire being as a single point of energy driving the breathing process. Then, open yourself. Think only of the entity you seek. Starting with the ghost's identity (if known), slowly expand your focus to include its personal history, the historical era of the ghost's death or creation of the emotional imprint, the reported nature and appearance of the haunting, and any specific ghostly activity.

Acknowledge each thought as you continue relaxed breathing. Find a thought that is most attractive to you, and then expand your mind to include your present surroundings. Return slowly to your current place and time. Remain quiet for a minute or two before you resume communication with your companions, then move ahead with the ghost hunt.

GROUP ORGANIZATION AND PREPARATION

It is not necessary to believe in spirits or paranormal phenomena in order to see a ghost or experience haunting activities. Indeed, most reports of ghost activities are made by unsuspecting people who never gave the matter much thought. But you should not include people in your group with openly negative attitudes about these things. If you include skeptics, be sure they maintain an open mind and are willing to participate in a positive group attitude.

Keep your group small, limited to four members if possible. Ghosts have been seen by large groups of people but small groups are more easily managed and likely to be of one mind in terms of objectives and methods.

Meet an hour or more prior to starting the ghost hunt at a location away from the site. Review the history of the ghost you seek and the previous reports of ghost activity at the site. Discuss the group's expectations based on known or suspected ghostly activity or specific research goals. Review possible audio and visual apparitions based on the history of paranormal activity at the site, telekinesis, local temperature changes, and intended methods of identifying or recording these phenomena. Most important, agree to a plan of action if a sighting is made by any member of the group.

The first priority for a ghost hunter is to maintain visual or auditory contact without a lot of activity such as making notes. Without breaking contact, do the following:

Activate recording devices.

Redirect audio, video, or photographic equipment to focus on the ghost.

Move yourself to the most advantageous position for listening or viewing the ghostly activity.

Attract the attention of group members with a code word, hand signal (for example, touch the top of your head), or any action that signals other hunters so they can pick up your focus of attention.

Should you attempt to interact with the ghost? Do so only if the ghost invites you to speak or move. Often, a ghost hunter's movement or noise frightens the ghost or interferes with the perception of the apparition.

SEARCHING FOR GHOSTS

There are no strict rules or guidelines for successful ghost hunting except BE PATIENT! Professional ghost hunters sometimes wait several days, weeks, even months before achieving contact with a ghost. Others have observed full-body apparitions when they least expected it, while concentrating fully on some other activity. Regardless of the depth of your research or preparation, you need to be patient. The serious ghost hunter will anticipate that several trips to a haunted site may be required before some sign of ghostly activity is observed.

If you hunt with a group, you need to establish a communications system in the event that even one member sights a ghost or experiences some evidence of ghostly activity. Of course, confirmation by a second person is important in establishing validity and credibility. In the previous section, a hand signal (hand to the top of the head) was recommended as a means of informing others that they should direct their eyes and ears to a site indicated by the person in contact with a ghost. Because of this, all ghost hunters need to keep their companions in sight at all times and be aware of hand signals.

An audio signal can often reduce the need for monitoring other ghost hunters for hand signals. Equally important for a group is to establish a method for calling other hunters who may be some distance away. Tugging on a length of string can be an effective signal. So can beeping devices, mechanical "crickets," and flashing penlight signals, i.e., one flash for a cold spot and two flashes for an apparition. Hand-held radios, or walkie-talkies, can also be effective. Some models can send an audio signal or activate flashing lights. Cell phones can be used, but the electromagnetic activity may be uninviting to your ghost.

Remaining stationary within a room, gravesite, courtyard, or other confirmed location is often most productive. If a ghost is known to have a favorite chair, bed, or other place within a room, he will appear. Under these conditions, the patient ghost hunter will have a successful hunt.

If your ghost is not known to appear at a specific place within a room or an outdoors area, position yourself to gain the broadest view of the site. A corner of a room is optimal because it allows the ghost unobstructed motion about the place while avoiding the impression of a trap set by uninvited people who occupy his favorite space. If you are outdoors at a gravesite, for instance, position yourself at the base of a tree or in the shadows of a monument to conceal your presence while affording a view of your ghost's grave.

If your ghost is a mobile spirit, moving throughout a house, over a bridge, or about a courtyard or graveyard, you may have no choice but to move around the area. Search for a place where you feel a change in the thickness of the air or a cold spot or detect a peculiar odor.

If you are ghost hunting with others, it may be advantageous to station members of your group at various places in the ghost's haunting grounds and use a reliable system to alert others to spirit activity. Each member could then patrol a portion of the site. Radio or cell phone communications may be essential for this type of ghost hunt.

Once you are on site, the above-described meditation may help you focus on and maintain empathy with your ghost. Investigate sounds, even common sounds, as the ghost attempts to communicate with you. Make mental notes of the room temperature, air movement, and the sensations of abrupt change in atmosphere as you move about the site. Changes in these factors may indicate the presence of a ghost.

Pay attention to your own sensations or perceptions, such as the odd feeling that someone is watching you, standing close by, or touching you. Your ghost may be hunting you!

WHAT TO DO WITH A GHOST

On occasion, professional ghost hunters make contact with a ghost by entering a trance and establishing two-way communications. The ghost hunter's companions hear him or her speak but the ghost's voice can only be heard by the trance communicator. Sylvia Browne's book, *Adventures of a Psychic,* describes several of these trance communication sessions. Most ghost encounters are brief, with little opportunity to engage the entity in conversation. But the ghost may make gestures or acknowledge your presence through eye contact, a touch on the shoulder, sound, or a movement of an object. The ghost hunter must decide whether or not to follow the gestures or direction of a ghost.

Visitors to the Gold Rush country's older wineries, mines, and historic buildings often feel the touch or tug of a ghost on their arm or shoulder. Spirits of deceased prospectors, miners, or outlaws may be trying to get living souls to notice them, move out of their way, or follow them to some important destination.

A ghost at Placerville's Union Cemetery, believed to be a veteran of the Civil War, points to the location of his grave. Many who have seen this ragged fellow wonder if he is trying get someone to open his coffin to retrieve valuables. A ghost at Coloma's Pioneer Cemetery wanders close to Cold Springs Road and waves to people driving by, beckoning them to follow her.

Phantom miners have been spotted on Prospector Road between Georgetown and Coloma and alongside Highway 108 near Jamestown. Those who have offered a ride to lifelike spirits were shaken when they disappeared from the passenger's seat, but they suffered no ill-effects.

In Volcano and Foresthill, the ghosts of Indian chiefs and shamans have appeared in several locations, including private homes, parks, vineyards, and inns. The menacing appearance of these tall spirits— sometimes dressed in colorful robes—has left some observers stunned and others scared out of their wits, but there are no reports of physical or psychological injury.

At the restored Nevada Theatre in Nevada City a male ghost creates an unpleasant atmosphere and dislikes sharing his favorite spaces with the living. To date, there are no credible or confirmed reports of lasting ill-effects by those who have been brave enough to have experienced contact with him.

The idea of a close experience with a ghost is frightening to most of us. More often, the ghost's activities are directed at getting the intruder to leave a room, house, or gravesite. If you sense your ghost wants you to leave, most hunters believe it is best not to push your luck. When you have established the nature of the ghost activity, ascertained that your companions have experienced the activity, taken a few photographs, and run a few minutes of audio tape it may be time to leave. An experience with an unfriendly ghost can be disturbing.

Residents of haunted houses and employees of haunted business establishments often accept a ghost's telekinetic or audio activities without concern. It is part of the charm of a place and may add some fun to working in a spooky building.

AFTER THE GHOST HUNT

Turn off all recorders and remove them to a safe place. Some ghost hunters suspect that ghosts can erase tapes. Label your tapes with the date, time, and location. Use a code number for each tape. Keep a separate record of where the tape was made, date, time, and contents. Place tapes in a waterproof bag with your name, address, telephone number and a note that guarantees postage in case it is misplaced. Have photographic film developed at a professional color laboratory. Pros at the lab may help you with cropping and image enhancement. Have copies made of the negatives that contain ghostly images.

All members of the group should meet right after the hunt, away from the site. Each hunter who witnessed ghostly activity or apparition should make a written or audio statement describing the experience. The form presented in Appendix A should be completed by the group leader. Video and audio recordings made at the site should be reviewed and reconciled with witness statements. Then, plans should be made for a follow-up visit in the near future to the site to confirm the apparition, its nature and form, and the impressions of the initial ghost hunt.

Data about the ghost's location within a site may indicate the optimal conditions for future contact. Things to be aware of include the time of day or night, phase of the moon, season, degree and size of cold spots, and the form and density of the apparition. Patience and detailed records can help you to achieve the greatest reward for a ghost hunter, unmistakable proof of ghostly activity.

CHAPTER 2

Gateways to the Gold Rush Country:
Sacramento, Folsom, and Stockton

As gold seekers trekked inland from coastal cities to the Sierra foothills they encountered settlements and villages that offered refuge, materials for repair of their wagons and equipment, fresh supplies, and valuable information about weather, routes to the gold diggings, and the latest gold discoveries. By 1852, these settlements were important centers of commerce, enriching storekeepers, local farmers, craftsmen (such as blacksmiths), and builders. Much of the gold extracted from the Sierras was transported to banks established in these new cities. Upon returning from the gold diggings, many miners settled in Sacramento, Folsom, and Stockton. Their newfound wealth broadened the economic base of these towns by investment in agriculture and other industries, fostering their transformation into important cities.

GHOST OF THE RICH MAN'S SON

Leland Stanford Mansion
800 N Street
Sacramento 95814
916-324-0575
www.stanfordmansion.org

More than one ghost may show up in this ornate mansion built in 1856 by merchant Shelton Fogus with profits from his Gold Rush businesses. The first sighting was recorded in 1885 by Governor Leland Stanford, Sr., after he witnessed the ghost of his son, Leland, Jr. There may be many other spirits in this beautiful but spooky place emanating from its checkered past.

The ghost of Governor Leland Stanford's son has appeared walking the halls of this grand mansion.

Leland Stanford might have remained a small town lawyer in Port Washington, Wisconsin if, in 1852, two momentous events had not occurred within hours of each other. During the night, a fire swept through part of town destroying his tiny office and small but invaluable law library. The next morning, Leland received a letter from his two brothers in Sacramento, California. In it, the brothers described the wealth they had accumulated by selling hardware to gold seekers. Facing ruin in Port Washington, Leland packed his bags and headed to New York where he boarded a ship for California.

Arriving almost penniless, Leland's brothers introduced him to Gold Rush country businessmen who helped him open a store in the Sierra foothills town of Michigan Bluff. Among these men were hardware dealers Mark Hopkins and Collis Huntington and dry goods merchant Charles Crocker. Success soon followed, and Leland became known as a fair and reasonable businessman. Being a lawyer, he was pressed into service as Justice of the Peace and became politically active, helping to form the Republican Party in California. By 1860, Leland was a wealthy political leader active in Abraham Lincoln's presidential campaign. In 1861, he partnered with his friends, Huntington, Crocker, and Hopkins, to form the Central Pacific Railroad. After accumulating enormous wealth and power, these men were later known throughout the West as the "Big Four." With their unlimited political and financial support, Leland was elected governor of California in 1862.

In 1861, anticipating his election as governor, Leland and his wife, Jane, purchased the Fogus home, believing that it was grand enough to be California's first gubernatorial mansion. They enlarged it from 4,000 square feet to more than 19,000 square feet and outfitted the place with the best art and furniture money could buy. After Leland left office, the Stanfords remained in the house, leaving succeeding governors to find their own gubernatorial mansions.

Late in 1883, while traveling in Italy, Stanford's son, Leland, Jr., contracted typhoid fever. He received the best medical care available but died March 13, 1884. Devastated by the loss of their only child, the Stanfords returned to their Sacramento mansion and shut themselves off from society. One night, while Governor Stanford sat alone in his study, the ghost of Leland, Jr. visited his father. The story goes that young Leland prevailed upon his father's altruism and interest in education, asking that a school of higher learning be established for young men. Astonished at the apparition of his dead son, the senior Leland followed his son's desire and dedicated the rest of his life to the creation of one of the nation's leading universities, Stanford University in Palo Alto, California.

In 1900, seven years after the death of Leland, Sr., Jane Stanford sold the mansion and, for the next ninety years it was used for philanthropic services. It was an orphanage, a home for high school girls who were about to become mothers, and a neighborhood settlement house. During these many years, something may have happened at this house that led to a haunting by the ghost of a short, thin, middle-aged woman. Recent experiences by ghost hunters suggest this ghost, who looks like a servant or nurse, walks the upper halls of the Stanford Mansion.

THE NOISY MANSION

Old Governor's Mansion
1526 H Street
Sacramento 95814
916-323-3047
www.parks.ca.gov

Built by Uriah Reese in 1877 as a private residence for Albert and Clemenza Gallatin, this mansion is the most spectacular example of 19th-century architecture in Sacramento. In 1903, the 16,000-square-foot mansion was purchased by the State of California as a home for Governor George Pardee, his wife Helen, and their four daughters. Thirteen California governors have resided there, but the beauty of the place, its rich furnishings, and ample luxuries never compensated for a variety of discomforts, including odd noises that disturbed the peace. In 1967, Nancy Reagan called the place a "fire trap" and pressured her husband, Ronald, to establish an executive residence elsewhere. Today, the mansion is accessible to the public by guided tour only, but the surrounding gardens and other buildings on the grounds offer opportunities for ghost hunters to investigate the premises.

The six-story-tall, gabled tower, mansard roof, and heavily decorated eaves, widow frames, and porches give the impression that this place must house a few ghosts. According to official records, though, only one death occurred there. Kate Olsen, wife of Governor Culbert Olsen, died in April of 1939 in the master bedroom. Ghost hunters who have visited the place doubt that her ghost is responsible for the paranormal activity that has been going on here for decades. They have concluded that the most active ghost is a young male who enjoys playing tricks on the living by hiding small objects and moving drawers.

When I first visited the mansion, I was only twelve years old. I accompanied my aunt, who was secretary to Governor Goodwin Knight, as she delivered a packet of personal mail to the governor. In awe of the huge house, as soon as I stepped inside I got a creepy feeling that some unseen being was watching me. Standing just inside the second foyer, I got a scary chill and felt as though a tall person had walked up behind me and hovered over the back of my neck. Almost too scared to look over my shoulder, I was relieved when my aunt's business was concluded. Pressing close to her, we turned and walked out, and those creepy feelings immediately left me. I returned many years later for a tour and found the place just as beautiful but still spooky.

Since the early thirties, the governor's mansion has been known as a place where strange, unexplained noises disturb its occupants. The son of Governor Warren often heard disembodied footsteps outside his bedroom door. Docents who have worked in the mansion have heard similar sounds in the same location. Sighs, closing doors, moving drawers, and shuffling sounds have been heard. In the 1970s, so many objects were being moved around without explanation that a park ranger spent several nights in the house hoping to catch a prankster. Nothing was seen, but the ranger reported several strange sounds. Writer Randall Reinstedt described a visit by two psychics from the San Francisco area who claimed they conversed with several ghosts who haunt the building.

One state employee reported the sensation of an unseen being passing close behind, a sensation reminiscent of my own experience in the foyer. Another employee reported that she was grabbed on the buttocks. In December of 2007, I found no docents who were willing to discuss the issue of ghosts in the mansion. Ghost hunters who tour the place are not allowed to do flash photography. An EMF meter or audio recorder for EVP may be used without arousing the indignation of docents, however.

CROWDED WITH GHOSTS

Old City Cemetery
1000 Broadway
Sacramento 95818
916-264-5621
www.oldcitycemetery.com

Prior to 1850, Sutter's Fort was the hub of the Sacramento settlement. Those who died at the fort were buried nearby in cemeteries that were recognizable only by weathered wooden grave markers. Frequent floods, blazing-hot summers, and damp, foggy winters caused rapid decay and destruction of these monuments resulting in discretion of the graves by grazing animals and expansion of Sutter's settlement. Recognizing the problem, Captain Sutter donated ten acres of high ground as a formal cemetery. Upon its opening late in 1850, many graves were relocated there from burial grounds near the fort. Over the years, additional donations of land were made until 1880 when Margaret Crocker donated the final ten acres, expanding the cemetery's holdings to sixty acres. As the city grew up around the cemetery, its

Sacramento's old City Cemetery contains the remains of more than 25,000 people, including pioneers, heroes, and many disaster victims.

grounds were reduced to the present total of 44 acres, containing over 25,000 graves. The location of this cemetery on the highest ground in Sacramento served to preserve the graves from flooding and inspire people to erect some fantastic monuments.

Among the first to be interred there were 600 victims of the cholera epidemic that struck the city in 1850. Special groups established exclusive burial grounds for their members. These include the Volunteers Fireman's plot, Grand Army plot, Old Masonic Cemetery, Odd Fellows section, Spanish-American War Veterans plot, and the pioneer section. The cemetery also houses the remains of the Donner party survivors, some of the region's early political leaders, and many important pioneers, including the son of Captain John Sutter. Ornate monuments, beautiful foliage, and the fascinating histories of those interred here make this necropolis a fascinating place for history buffs and ghost hunters alike.

Some professional ghost hunters and writers argue that cemeteries are not good places to search for spiritual entities or other paranormal phenomena. I disagree. Residual energy or environmental imprints created by the intense emotions of a funeral can be detected at a gravesite decades after the burial. This is particularly true if a family member renews that emotional imprint by making frequent visits to the site. Ghosts of the deceased may show up in a cemetery if an error was made in the burial, such as being placed in the wrong grave, or they wish to have some other problem resolved. Ghosts of a parent may travel within a cemetery to watch over the graves of their child. Finally, a ghost may show up if its grave marker was lost, destroyed, or covered by a parking lot, road, or other structure.

Local ghost hunters have identified at least six ghosts that haunt the old City Cemetery. The ghost that scares people the most is that of a dog. This creature shows up during tours of the cemetery led by historians and psychics. It is reported that the sound of animal nails on concrete is audible before the apparition is seen. The dog is described as a large, muscular pit bull. It is not threatening, but its sudden appearance inside the fenced cemetery unnerves people. Ghost hunters can get within 15 feet of this apparition before it disappears.

The ghost of William Brown, known in life as the African-American Casey Jones, appears wearing the clothing of a train engineer, complete with signature cap. William wanders from his grave, showing up in the Hamilton Square section of the cemetery. It is said that this ghost is looking for the person responsible for his death. In 1880, William was the engineer on a train speeding toward San Francisco Bay. A switchman failed to throw the switch, sending William's train onto the wrong track and into the chilly water. Seeing the unavoidable disaster that loomed ahead, Brown calmly uncoupled the cars behind the coal tender, saving hundreds of lives.

The ghost of a fireman stands near the gate of the Volunteer Fireman's plot. Psychics have spoken to this ghost and learned that he is searching for members of his family. When told they are all dead, he gets angry and walks away. This fellow may be confused by the distinction between life and death because he died quickly and unexpectedly when he was decapitated by a train trestle.

The ghost of a little girl dressed in a party dress wanders among the larger monument near the front gate. She doesn't speak to the living, but her singing can be heard and captured on audio recorders. She may have died in one of the epidemics that ravaged Sacramento in the 1850s.

A man and woman dressed in black mourning clothes have appeared at docent-led tours with as many as 200 people milling about. They appear so lifelike that one might think they were merely dressed in period costumes to add historical elements to special tours. These folks even pose for photographs, but they cannot be seen when the images are reviewed.

Fascinating stories about the cemetery's residents that may serve as a basis for further research and successful ghost hunts can be accessed online. Go to the archives of the Sacramento Bee and access Gina Kim's October 31, 2006, article. You will find intriguing information about some outrageous characters, their deaths, and reasons why they may haunt the old City Cemetery.

SUTTER'S FORT

2701 L Street
Sacramento 95816
916-445-4422
www.parks.ca.gov

The spirit of the old west lives on at Sutter's Fort State Park, making it a great location for ghost hunting. The fort was established in 1841 by Swiss immigrant Captain John Augustus Sutter, at a time when most of central California was wild country in the hands of Indians. With a Mexican land grant of 150,000 acres, Sutter envisioned a great outpost at the confluence of the American and Sacramento Rivers. Ever mindful of the region's political instability and military vulnerabilities, he constructed a fort with thick walls of adobe, heavy gates, and towers armed with cannon. Known as New Helvetia, Sutter's Fort became an agricultural and manufacturing center that flourished by attracting skilled Indian and Mexican workers. They were also attracted by Sutter's reputation for generosity and hospitality to weary travelers and indigenous people. Among the famous visitors who sojourned at Sutter's Fort are Kit Carson, the great frontiersman and trapper, and Colonel John Charles Fremont, who led one of the first American military ventures into the Mexican province of Alta in 1846.

After the Bear Flag Revolt of 1846 and the annexation of California by America, the fort became a hub, an essential stopping point for American military units and immigrants entering the territory. In November of 1846, several rescue parties were formed at the fort and dispatched to the ill-fated Donner party trapped by early snows in the high Sierras. In March and April of 1847, several survivors arrived at

Established in Sacramento in 1841, Sutter's Fort was an oasis for explorers and early immigrants suffering the hardships of the California wilderness and portal to the primitive Gold Rush Country from civilized America.

the fort where they told tales of horrific miseries and cannibalism. An artifact of the Donner party—a tiny doll—is on display at the fort.

Sutter's greatest fame derives from his luck and wisdom in hiring James Marshall to build a sawmill on the middle fork of the American River. It was Marshall's discovery of gold that opened the gates of California to hundreds of thousands of gold seekers from all over the world, many of whom rested and re-supplied at Sutter's Fort. The first gold nuggets discovered by Marshall were cast upon Sutter's desk in a room open to the public.

Throughout the 1840s and early 1850s, the fort flourished, attracting many Indians, politically disenfranchised Mexicans, sick and injured gold seekers, and Yankees who were disillusioned by their failure to find gold and the hardships of California's wilderness. At times, a large village of tents, lean-tos, and broken wagons surrounded the fort and housed hundreds. Many of those who sought shelter in this crowded village died there of injuries and disease, including cholera, typhoid, and yellow fever. In some cases, burial was haphazard and the graves unmarked. In 2006, a grave was discovered under L Street when a sewer was rebuilt. Several artifacts indicated that the remains dated from the late 1840s. Historians and ghost hunters suspect many undiscovered deposits of human remains and artifacts underground, both inside and outside the fort's walls.

Many victims of the cholera epidemic of the early 1850s were sequestered in the fort's east tower. So many people died in this space that sensitive people often detect great misery there. This is a good spot to use divining rods or attempt orb photography.

DELTA KING RIVERBOAT

Old Sacramento Waterfront
1000 Front Street
Sacramento 95814
916-995-5464
www.deltaking.com

Virtually all ships are haunted. A lingering ghost onboard old ships is practically a tradition, borne out of the tendency of sailors to harbor superstition, rely on supernatural powers for guidance and protection, and attribute blame to someone beyond themselves when something goes wrong. The Delta King riverboat, berthed at the riverfront pier in Old Sacramento, has at least one ghost. Based on his uniform and the places he appears, he has been identified as a former captain. An Internet source reports that he appears in the ship's balcony during theatrical productions and walks the upper deck, a place usually reserved for officers. This report contains at least one error, but the true identify of

From 1927 to the late 1930s, the Delta King carried passengers between Sacramento and San Francisco Bay in unfettered luxury.

this ghost may be discerned by reviewing the history of this famous ship.

The 285-foot Delta King and its sister ship, the Delta Queen, were launched on May 20, 1927. Designed to carry passengers between San Francisco and Sacramento in eight to ten hours, the over-night trip was a veritable party, with fine dining, gambling, dancing, and legal consumption of alcohol during the Prohibition era (1920-1933). The decadent mode of travel attracted high society along with thieves, gangsters, and con men.

These magnificent riverboats continued service until the late 1930s when better roads and bridges and reliable automobiles provided a more convenient and faster means of travel between the two cities. During WWII, both ships were used on San Francisco Bay as floating barracks, hospital ships, and anti-submarine net tenders. Eventually, the Delta Queen was towed to New Orleans, where she was outfitted for the tourist trade on the Mississippi River. The Delta King sank in the mud of San Francisco Bay and was left derelict for many years. In 1984, the ship was raised and underwent a five-year renovation before returning to its Sacramento berth. Today, the Delta King serves as a waterfront hotel with a first-rate theatre and stands as a reminder of the importance of river travel to the development of Sacramento.

Since the ship's theatre has no balcony, Internet reports of ghostly activity in that location are necessarily in error. However, the ghost of a distinguished looking man, dressed in a dark blue suit with brass buttons, has been spotted in the last row of the theatre. The same apparition, wearing a hat, has been seen walking the upper deck. At times, his coat looks short, in a cut-away style, resembling a jacket that might be worn by a waiter. This fellow may have been a live-aboard employee who never knew a more pleasant home than the Delta King. The best way to investigate this ghost is to spend a night aboard the ship or attend a theatrical performance.

HOME OF THE MADAME OF MURDER

Dorothea Puente House
1426 F Street
Sacramento 95814

This aged Victorian house blends in with its neighbors, but the veil of misery and horror that hangs over it is easily detected by sensitive ghost hunters. In the 1980s, Dorothea Puente operated the place as a board-and-care facility for disabled elderly, many of them alcoholics. After gaining the confidence of her tenants, and their distant relatives, she murdered them, then living off their social security checks and other monthly income. Puente was eventually convicted of murdering eight people, but police investigators believe the true number of victims may exceed twenty-four. Many of the deaths that occurred at the Puente house were attributed to natural causes and not questioned by coroners or mortuary staff because the deceased had a history of multiple chronic illnesses. However, given Puente's penchant for poison and lack of oversight by victims' relatives, it appears that Dorothea was a busy little murderess between 1982 and 1988, during which period she killed most of her tenants.

Suspicions about Dorothea's activities were first aroused in 1986 when Dorothea's live-in boyfriend, Malcolm McKenzie, disappeared under suspicious circumstances. His body was later discovered inside a crude, homemade casket floating in the Sacramento River. Two years later, Dorothea's neighbors called the police to report the bizarre activity of Puente's handyman, a man known as "Chief." Chief had been observed carting soil away, tearing up the basement concrete floor, and dismantling the detached garage. After several months of work, Dorothea ordered Chief to pour a fresh slab of cement in the backyard. When the job was completed, Chief disappeared.

On November 11, 1988, police found a body buried only a few inches deep under the lawn in Puente's backyard. Soon, crime-scene investigators uncovered the remains of seven more victims. Dorothy Miller, 65, was found buried in the backyard with her arms bound to her chest with duct tape. Leona Carpenter, 78, was found buried near the back fence. Her leg bone was initially thought to be a tree root. When the body of Vera Faye Martin, 64, was unearthed, her wristwatch was still ticking. The only body recovered from the grounds at the front of the house was that of Betty Palmer, 78. Betty was buried near the front sidewalk, beneath a statue of St. Francis of Assisi. Clad in a white nightgown, her hands, head, and lower legs were missing.

According to local ghost hunter and writer Paul Dale Roberts, Haunted and Paranormal Investigations (HPI) member Cherie

Vincent obtained a fascinating EVP while standing outside the house. On her audio recording, a male voice said, "I don't want to be here." I performed an EVP sweep at the front of the house, aiming my microphone at the small patch of ground where Betty Palmer's remains were recovered. I heard nothing, but two EVPs were found during the playback of my digital recorder. The first was a female voice that said "Oh, no." I could not identify the gender of the second voice; it sounded husky and the words were quite slurred. My best analysis suggests the EVP contained "Find me."

Roberts concludes that the Puente house is not haunted but merely a curious urban legend. Not long ago, the house was blessed and cleansed of any lingering spirits. While the place may be cleared of spirits, it is likely that many intense environmental imprints remain that may create EVP, generate light anomalies in photographs, and attract the attention of sensitive ghost hunters. It would be hard to imagine how Dorothea Puente's evil and the misery of her tenants could be dissipated by the passage of only two decades. Added to that, police are not certain there aren't more bodies under the house or buried deeper in the backyard.

A GHOST NAMED PINKY

Sacramento Theatre Company
1419 H Street
Sacramento 95814
916-443-6722
www.sactheatre.org

Most theatres are haunted by ghosts of performers or directors whose spirits could not leave the place where passion and creativity took them to the pinnacle of their lives. Sometimes, theatres are haunted by star-struck members of the audience who came night after night to see a performer who aroused them romantically or sexually. Stagehands also haunt theatres after a sudden, tragic death caused by falling from the catwalks or being crushed by falling scenery or stage equipment. Investigations of haunted theatres often reveal a history of suicide by performers whose careers were failing, murder by jealous rivals, or bizarre crimes committed by stalkers. Some paranormal activity discovered in theatres is simply residual energy or environmental imprints of intense emotion created by performers, who experienced horrific stage fright or extreme elation after a great performance. In some cases paranormal activity was created by performers who were angered by rivals, their personal failures, or audiences who jeered instead of cheered.

The building that houses the Sacramento Theatre Company has not been the scene of suicide, murder, or headline crimes such as often lead to ghostly activity or a haunting, but still the place is haunted. The ghost of a man has been spotted there so often that members of the theatre company have named him "Pinky." The odd name was chosen because the ghost manifests by creating a pink aura or light anomaly. Another male ghost named Joe shows up in one of the dressing rooms. It is believed that Joe used to assist with various theatre productions. A failed actress haunts the women's dressing room. Her sadness generates an atmosphere of misery and despair.

The theatre is composed of the Main Stage, with seating for three hundred, and Stage Two, with seat for ninety. In the 1990s, psychics examined the entire building and discovered at least five spirits haunting it. They offered no explanation for intense ghostly activity in a building constructed in 1949. The nature of the theatrical experience—for performers, creative staff, and ardent theatre fans—may be sufficient explanation. None of the ghosts in this building appear to be from an era before the building was constructed. The best way to begin an investigation of ghosts in this place is to attend a performance. Make the acquaintance of staff members who may be able to grant access after-hours.

CALIFORNIA STATE LIBRARY

914 Capitol Mall
Sacramento 95814
916-654-0176 (History Room)
e-mail: clscal@library.ca.gov

Librarians are known for their passion. They are passionate about books, manuscripts, and old periodicals, especially if these comprise special collections, such as diaries of survivors of the Donner party tragedy. Those who are passionate are usually protective, and so it is that old libraries are often haunted by librarians who cannot bear to leave cherished books and special collections behind. The California State Library has several ghosts linked to the place by the vast collection of documents, pictorial materials, photographs, and ephemera such as posters and sheet music, much of which dates from the Gold Rush era.

Some of the ghosts in this library are devoted readers and researchers who would not let death tear them away from their private passion or interrupt their search for an elusive book or diary that would complete their research. At least two ghosts, a man and a woman, are believed to be former librarians. Most sightings are made in the California History section. The most frequently sighted apparition is that of a tall, elderly man who wears glasses. I first saw this fellow at the age of twelve when I visited the library with my aunt. I noticed he wore heavy, dark clothing with a shiny black bow tie, and looked quite different from the other men who browsed the stacks of books. In later

The ghosts of dedicated librarians and historians roam the hallways of the California State Library in Sacramento.

visits, I saw this man walk among the stacks, appearing completely lifelike, and then disappear as he turned a corner. Recently I found a Web site that included photographs of prior State librarians. Flipping through the pages, I was amazed to discover that Robert O. Craven was the ghost I had seen. Craven was appointed State Librarian in 1870 and served for 12 years. On January 10, 1917, he died at the age of 89.

The female ghost seen at the library may be that of Mabel Gillis. The library career of this accomplished woman spanned 47 years, with 21 years as State Librarian. Mabel died on September 6, 1961, a few days short of her 79th birthday.

The ghosts of several library patrons with an affinity for the California History Section show up often. Ghost hunters and visitors report hearing footfalls in an adjacent isle only to find no one there. Books sometimes move by unseen hands. Paul Dale Roberts lists the California State Library as one of the ten most haunted locations in Sacramento.

FOLSOM HOTEL

703 Sutter Street
Folsom 95630
916-985-2530

Virtually every building that sits on Folsom's historic Sutter Street has a ghost story associated with it. The Folsom Hotel is the locale most often visited by ghost hunters and tourists looking for a paranormal thrill. Opened in 1857, the hotel has retained the look of a Gold Rush era bar, gambling hall, and flophouse. Rustic wood doors, floors, and original bar contribute a lot to the old west atmosphere and block the intrusion of the 21st century. The long and sordid past of the building is not easy to uncover, but bartenders and locals perched on bar stools told me stories of the hotel's wild days that occurred in the 1860s, 1880s, 1920s, and late 1940s. They also told me a few ghost stories.

The prized paranormal remnant of the Folsom Hotel is a five by seven inch photograph snapped Christmas Eve of 2005. The photo captured six people caught up in the celebration, but it also captured

Ghosts from the Gold Rush days still patronize the bar in the Folsom Hotel.

the image of a man nobody knew. A few days after Christmas, the picture was circulated among the bar's regulars. No one knew the bearded man whose face appears clearly at the left border of the picture. Added to that, everyone was certain they did not see this man at the party. Finally, an old-timer volunteered that the fellow looked like the man who installed new mirrors on the back bar 20 years earlier. It was recalled that the man worked for days installing the mirrors and doing other repairs. When the job was finished, he stepped up to the bar to admire his work and enjoy a tall drink on the house. After finishing the drink, he slipped off the barstool and dropped dead on the floor.

Bartenders also told me stories about the ghosts of the second floor. Rooms are no longer rented by the night, but the renters who occupy the hotel's eight rooms often report ghostly shadows, cold spots, unexplained odors, and missing objects that turn up in bizarre places. The most active ghost on the second floor is believed to be that of a woman who died in the building. Referring to room four, former hotel worker Anita Brown said, "I can tell you that there are ghosts in there." She often felt "a presence or coldness, like there was definitely something there." The identity of this ghost remains unknown, but is it most likely that she was a prostitute or housekeeper.

The male ghost of the Folsom Hotel has been named "Doc." Reba Poole, a regular customer and frequent performer in the bar, said the electrical supply to her band's equipment often fails or acts up. "I personally have seen some filmy presence . . . and [sometimes] catch a glimpse of him out of the corner of my eye." Thinking the band's electrical problems were caused by Doc, Reba began leaving chocolates for him. The sweet offerings apparently appeased the ghost, because the band can now play a full set without power problems.

The second floor of the Folsom Hotel is accessible only to monthly renters unless you contact the building's manager in advance. The Folsom Hotel enjoys its ghostly legacy and welcomes ghost hunters to roam around the place enjoying the ambience and spirits of the 1860s.

COHN MANSION

305 Scott Street
Folsom 95630
www.wsjhistory.com/cohn_mansion_folsom_ca.htm

Built in the early 1890s by California State Senator Phillip C. Cohn (1854-1928), this house incorporated an 1860 cabin into its structure. The cabin now serves as the kitchen. Local ghost hunters believe the place is haunted. For decades, reports circulated around Folsom that disembodied footsteps and ghostly images were experienced on a regular basis by the residents of the house.

The grand mansion stands on a hill overlooking Folsom's historic Sutter Street. Exterior and interior renovations are underway, but the place has a sad appearance, with many original features, such as the etched glass on the twin front doors, showing the wear of more than a century. A local merchant told me that three lawyers purchased the house more than five years ago with the intention of converting it into a law office. Others in the neighborhood said the work on

Senator Phillip C. Cohn built this mansion, which would later become a house of many secrets, in the 1890s.

the conversion moves ahead at a very slow pace and that something frequently stalls workmen. Looking through the windows of the first floor, I saw that the double parlors were nearing completion. The house was empty, but as I looked through the windows of the double parlors I heard strange knocking sounds that seemed to originate from these rooms. Digital images taken here did not reveal orbs or other light anomalies. A neighbor told me that lights are often seen in the tower windows late at night while the rest of the house is dark.

The ghostly activity that was experienced by the Cohn family in the 1890s may be linked to a bizarre discovery. Karen Mehring, director of the Folsom History Museum, reported that, many years ago, during reconstruction of the front steps, the skeleton of an 18-month old child was found under the porch. Wrapped in a blanket and housed in a wooden box, the mystery was never solved. Since the Cohn family occupied this house from 1892 to 1966, this grizzly discovery may be all that remains of a tragedy that could have become a scandal.

THE EIGHT BALL GHOST

Yagers Tap House and Grill
727 Trader Lane
Folsom 95630
916-985-4677

The building that houses this popular watering hole is an enigmatic remnant of the Gold Rush days. The details of its history have been lost in the passing of one and a half centuries, but it is likely that it served many roles in the booming town, including boarding house and gambling hall. It is a virtual certainty that it was once a miners' drinking establishment and the upstairs rooms housed more than a few ladies of the evening. Prominently situated on historic Sutter Street, the businesses housed in this building rode the tides of flush times and recessions. The rapid turnover of businesses that probably involved the loss of many fortunes, and a few lives, may underlie the ghostly phenomena that occur at Yagers Tap House.

When I visited the building in 2007, I was impressed by the architectural achievement that placed this enduring structure on a steep hillside facing the American River. The four floors of the Tap House are stacked and staggered, interconnected by steep stairs. As I descended from the street-level floor to the lowest level, I felt increasingly cut-off from the modern era and more in touch with the palpable atmosphere of the 19th century. My digital camera failed to capture orbs, but bizarre shadows became more prominent as I moved lower in the building.

One of the recent ghostly events at this place, reported by a bartender to writer Jamie Trump (*Folsom Telegraph,* October 25, 2005), indicates a spirit's affinity for pool. While opening the establishment one morning, an eight ball was discovered to be missing. A thorough search by the entire staff failed to locate it. Later that night, while closing the place, a manager passed near the pool table when the eight ball rolled across the floor and struck his foot. On many occasions, other balls turned up missing for a day or so only to be found on or near the pool table.

Other ghostly occurrences in the place include icy cold spots in some of the booths, whispers overheard by patrons while they were alone in the restrooms, and that creepy sensation that someone is standing close behind you. The spirits of this place may be linked to three mysterious caves or tunnels that used to open into the bottom floor. They are now blocked with sheets of steel, but ghosts have been known to pass through stronger barriers.

GHOST OF THE UNSEEN COMPANION

St. John the Baptist Catholic Church Cemetery
Natoma Street at Sibley Street
Folsom 95630
916-985-2065
http://saintjohnsfolsom.ca.campusgrid.net/home

The church that stands over this desolate, seemingly forgotten cemetery was built in 1857. An antique photograph found on the church's website shows the place looking just as it does today but surrounded by a broad field of grass. Sibley Street now cuts across that field and runs close to the church's east wall. In the picture a short picket fence encloses the small graveyard, which, at that time, was already the final resting-place of several local pioneers. Today, the church stands in good repair, thanks to devoted parishioners who still use the place for weddings and other special religious events. Portions of the picket fence still stand, too, but it has been supplemented by a sturdy cast iron fence that was stylish during the latter half of the 19th century.

A walk around a graveyard in broad daylight usually does not lead to brushes with the paranormal, but at St. John's Baptist Cemetery that rule does not apply. As soon as I entered the gate, I got the impression that an unseen spirit had descended the nearby church steps and

The graveyard surrounding St. John's Baptist Church, in Folsom, is full of spirits who create EVP.

moved close to me. The bizarre sensation of a close, unseen entity persisted until I left the cemetery forty-five minutes later. Many ghost hunters who visit this place enjoy memorable encounters with spirits. Ghost hunters from HPI have visited this cemetery many times and reported several EVP and photographic evidence of ghostly activity. Ghost hunter Cherie Vincent has collected several EVP at the grave of Domingoes Brum (1882-1979). One EVP, recorded by Cheri at the grave, features the ghost's clearly audible remark, "I know you." Writer Paul Dale Roberts asked this entity to touch him. The response was a burning sensation on his thigh, followed by the deep impression of a thumbprint. At the grave of Frank Antonio, EVPs have included "I miss you" and "Alright." Another grave that often yields good EVP is that of Daniel A. Lowney, a veteran of WWI.

As I walked around the cemetery, picking up an occasional EVP of less than desirable quality, my unseen companion pressed close at times, creating the distinct impression that a tall, muscular person was trying to push me in the direction of the cemetery's gate. Stepping away from the entity, I snapped a few digital images but found no light anomalies. As I approach the gate on Sibley Street, I felt the entity step away. Curious about this spirit, and wishing to get a photograph of the graveyard church's porch, I climbed the steps only to encounter the tall, robust being pressing close once again. I took this as an invitation to leave.

Who was this unseen escort? Looking back through the church's history, I found that a long line of Irish priests served the church beginning at its foundation. I believe that perhaps the ghost of one of these men noticed that I am Irish and was trying to get my attention.

LAKESIDE CEMETERY AND MAUSOLEUM

Natoma Street at Folsom Boulevard
Folsom 95630
916-985-2295

Shaded by tall oaks and cedars, this cemetery sprawls over a hundred acres. Graves seemed to be placed in groups, resembling little island cemeteries on a sea of green grass. Many of the monuments are covered with foliage that has not been tamed by gardeners or relatives of the deceased. The result is a spooky ambience, even in broad daylight. Local ghost hunting groups visit this cemetery often, because it has a reputation as a good venue for EVP work. HPI writer Paul Dale Roberts offers reports of EVP sweeps in his Internet articles posted at www.hauntedamericatours.com. His EVP findings at this location include such fascinating audio recordings as "we are above the trees" and "take me away." Roberts even reports an EVP of a ghost mocking him by repeating phrases laced with profanity. One male spirit, who apparently saw the divining rods, also known as dowsing rods, carried by ghost hunters, created an EVP in which he asked, "What are those?"

In addition to audio recorders, ghost hunters have used dowsing rods to detect the presence of entities. During a joint investigation of Lakeside Cemetery, both Vincent and Roberts held dowsing rods over 12 graves while they asked the gender of the deceased entombed within. According to Roberts, the rods moved in a way that correctly identified the deceased's gender 11 times. From eight different locations within the cemetery, these dowsing rods also consistently pointed to a single grave popularly believed to be haunted.

When I learn of reports such as this, I always wonder why a spirit would haunt a graveyard rather than his home or workplace. Writer Troy Taylor believes that ghosts who haunt graveyards are a different type of spirit altogether. These ghosts are connected with the cemetery in some way that does not include events or activities in which they engaged when they were alive. Instead, something that occurred after death entices them to remain near a grave. Their body may be in the wrong grave. The name on the headstone may be misspelled or the epitaph may be incorrect, incomplete, or lack the glowing adjectives a ghost feels he deserves. Ghosts may stand watch over their graves if they have been desecrated or robbed, or if the headstone has been destroyed by natural disaster or vandalism.

During my visits to Lakeside Cemetery, I obtained no EVP or digital images with orbs, but I did encounter several graves surrounded by a bizarrely thickened atmosphere. In some cases the air felt much colder that that of adjacent areas. These graves had one interesting characteristic in common. The headstones were either broken or had become illegible. Ghost hunters who plan to visit Lakeside Cemetery may use this fascinating discovery to find a starting point for their own investigations.

SITE OF MASS GRAVES

Old State Insane Asylum
612 East Magnolia Street
Stockton 95202

Legends and myths about the old Stockton State Hospital are easy to find, although little is left of the historic insane asylum. Nearly all of the original buildings have been demolished, leaving most of the facility's 100 acres as open ground. Today, a few former clinic and support buildings, together with some new additions, comprise the fledgling campus of California State University Stanislaus. Stately Victorian mansions once occupied by the hospital's superintendent and doctors still stand on East Acacia Street, a reminder of the hospital facility's once-great size and the power its staff held over the lives of thousands of patients. To some people, the almost Gothic appearance of these buildings and other spooky remnants give credence to the legends and myths, including ghost stories. When visitors walk the grounds, the sad history of a place is inescapable.

Established in 1853 as the Insane Asylum of California, the facility grew larger each decade, eventually housing more than 3,000 patients in wards and dormitories. The facility was renamed the Stockton State Hospital in 1896 and subsequently closed a century later, in 1996. After closure, some of the older buildings stood vacant for a few years, serving as venues for local ghost hunters and thrill seekers. Some of the latter have published Internet tales of locked doors that lead to underground tunnels and "dead spots" on the grounds where a foul, vomit-like stench lingers. These tales might be dismissed as urban myths, but in 2005 several unmarked graves were uncovered on the old hospital grounds, leading to investigations by serious ghost hunters and designation of the grounds as a haunted site.

Since 2005, so many unmarked graves have been discovered on the old hospital grounds that researchers have raised questions about how many people remain buried at the site. Between 1854 and 1875, at the site of the women's facility, 510 E. Magnolia Street, 4,467 known burials were done. In 1876, 1,619 bodies were removed to another cemetery nearby on North California Street. More exhumations and reburials were done between 1925 and 1926, but the exact number is unclear. In any case, it seems clear that thousands of bodies of people who suffered from mental illness remain at the location. Graves of those who died at the facility were not marked with headstones. Wooden markers that indicated graveyard boundaries were burned away in the 1950s by grass fires.

In May of 2007, another forgotten hospital cemetery was discovered at the end of East Acacia Street when workers broke ground for a retention pond. Initial reports indicated that 30 graves were found, but the true number is almost certainly much higher. When I visited the site in December of 2007, a chain-link fence protected the area. The sight of my camera attracted the attention of a security guard, who informed me that photography was forbidden without permission of the grounds supervisor. I found this odd, since I stood on public ground that was part of a university campus. After speaking to a representative of the grounds supervisor, I was given permission to take photos but informed that I could not publish them. I could not help but wonder if San Joaquin County's plans for further searches for unmarked graves has created a delicate atmosphere.

There are reports that students have heard disembodied voices, sobs, moans, and screams in some of the classroom buildings that were once used for treatments or as patients' dormitories. Disembodied footsteps have also been heard, and chairs have been seen moving across the floor without explanation. At the end of Acacia Street, on the former site of the women's facility on East Magnolia Street, sensitive ghost hunters pick up the intense misery, fear, anxiety, and desperation that must have been experienced by thousands of patient incarcerated here. Paranormal investigators who are skilled with dowsing rods locate hot spots indicating unmarked graves. Considering the long period of operation of the insane asylum and the intensity of emotion that occurred there, it would be astonishing if no residual energy remained on the old hospital grounds.

EVP HEAVEN

Stockton Rural Cemetery
2350 Cemetery Lane
Stockton 95204
209-465-5213

For ghost hunters traveling from the Bay Area to the Gold Rush country, Stockton is a good place for a rest stop. The city has everything travelers need, including a nice cemetery for talking a walk and soaking up some local history. Opened in 1862, when the area was some distance from the city's center, the Rural Cemetery contains the remains of pioneers, plus some interesting new additions such as Russ Meyer, producer of the cult films *Vixen* and *Beyond the Valley of the Dolls.* Under the summer sun, the place doesn't look too spooky, but when the place is shrouded by winter fog the grave markers and larger monuments take on an entirely different appearance, looking like a New Orleans necropolis. At night, when the fog drifts away and the graveyard is illuminated by moonlight accented by long shadows, the play of light on polished granite creates an eerie atmosphere as spirits leave EVP on audio recorders.

A fascinating EVP can be accessed on the website of the San Joaquin Valley Paranormal Investigators. Recorded on March 4, 2007, the high-pitched, male voice of can be heard repeating the word, "hi" as ghost hunters talk about the site. The tone of the voice suggests the disembodied speaker was trying to get the attention of living visitors. I do not know when the ghost hunters became aware of this EVP. If playback was done several minutes or hours later, an opportunity might have been missed for communication with a ghost. For this reason, I recommend that ghost hunters use audio devices that allow the user to monitor all audio input via headphones or playback every two to five minutes.

In the Rural Cemetery, a ghost has been spotted near the grave of Civil War veteran Peter Singleton Wilkes (block 21, lot 1, north half). The dark figure looks like a short person, standing only about five feet tall, draped in a black veil. This apparition appears just before dusk, stands over the grave as if praying, and then vanishes. Wilkes served in the Confederate Congress from 1864 to 1865 and then came West to Stockton, dying in 1900.

Other places to hunt ghosts in the gateway cities:

GHOST OF A VICTORIAN LADY

The Record Store
708 K Street Mall
Sacramento 95814

This once-popular record store is now closed. The building stands vacant and, through the windows, appears to be quite dirty. For years local ghost hunters listed this place as one of the most haunted sites in Sacramento. The most active ghost is that of a woman dressed in a black Victorian gown with a white, high collar. Both employees and customers spotted her when the store was still in operation. One customer complained to the manager that an oddly dressed "old lady" had asked her to leave the store. This ghost appeared so often that store employees named her Gertrude, and then became accustomed to using a nickname, Gertie. Gertie may be a remnant from the 1920s, when the building was a hotel. Aside from being a rare apparition in that it is detailed and nearly full length, Gertie also creates cold spots, moves lights around, and speaks.

The ghost of a young man has also been reported in the record store. This fellow appears to be a laborer in his twenties, wearing jeans and a heavy shirt. Ghost hunters may gain entry to the building by contacting the owner.

SACRAMENTO RIVER

Greenhaven Drive at Riverside Boulevard
Sacramento 95831

Many people have drowned in the Sacramento River as a result of floods, boating accidents, and poor judgment while swimming. Carefully walk up the levee and descent the embankment toward the river. Writer Paul Dale Roberts tells us to look for a campfire that appears, and then fades away. The odor of burning wood may be detected, too. It is believed that a homeless man used to camp in the area, bathe in the river, and then build a campfire for warmth through the night. Years ago, a man described as a transient was found drowned at this location. His ghost may haunt his favorite camping spot.

BURGER KING

7218 Stockton Boulevard (near Florin Road)
Sacramento 95823
916-393-0744

In 1997, a man entered this Burger King restaurant, wandered about among the customers as if he were waiting to meet someone, then walked behind the counter and shot the manager. To the horror of on-lookers, he then turned the gun on himself and ended his own life. Remnants of that horrible event remain. People working the late shift have reported to local ghost hunters that they have heard gunshots and screams when the restaurant is nearly empty. On November 24, 2007, I questioned day shift staff about the incident and possible paranormal events in the building. They denied any knowledge of the shooting or ghostly activity.

SAND COVE PARK

2101 Garden Highway
Unincorporated Sacramento County
916-264-5200

Ghostly lights are alleged to appear at this popular Sacramento River park at night. EVP have been recorded here, too; the voice of a woman has been recorded saying "Te papa." Local ghost hunters suspect it was once an Indian burial ground, but it is more likely that any spirits roaming the area were victims of one of the many floods that plagued the lowlands adjoining the Sacramento River.

COUNTY COURTHOUSE

222 East Weber Avenue
Stockton 95202

The current courthouse sits on the site of the original municipal building constructed in 1853. It has been reported that in the basement of the building, in the holding cells for prisoners, janitors and sheriff's deputies have heard screams and shouts at times when all occupants are quiet. The sound of metal doors opening and closing has been reported, too. This portion of the building is not accessible to ghost hunters, but some staff members may be willing to share their experiences with serious researchers.

CHAPTER 3

The Northern Gold Diggings: Downieville, North San Juan, Nevada City, and Grass Valley

Early in 1849, when reports of James Marshall's discovery of gold at Sutter's Mill spread across the Sierra foothills, settlers already established on ranches and farms began digging up creek beds and picking at quartz outcroppings. With little effort, many of them gathered thousands of dollars in gold each day and used this newfound wealth to transform camps into boomtowns and cities. By 1851, the muddy encampment known as Deer Creek Diggings had become Nevada City, complete with sidewalks, stylish hotels and restaurants, several banks, and mansions erected by new millionaires. For a while, North San Juan, Downieville, and other northern Sierra towns also enjoyed rapid growth in population and wealth and expanded with fancy buildings and cultural institutions, such as theatres, operas, and schools. As miners moved to Sacramento and San Francisco to retire with their wealth many towns declined and, by the end of the 19th century, were so sparsely populated that they were known as ghost towns. Today, former boomtowns such as Nevada City, North San Juan, and Downieville are popular tourist destinations. Remnants of their wild days as Gold Rush towns remain in charming inns, cafes, stores, and historical points of interest.

GHOST OF JUANITA

Yuba River Bridge
Downieville 95936

The ghost of Juanita is perhaps the most fabled spirit in California's Gold Rush country. Her notoriety, which has grown into a kind of historical fame, is due to her unique fate. On a single day, July 5,

1851, this young Mexican woman killed a man, stood trial in front of hundreds of miners, and was hanged on the Jersey Bridge that spanned the Yuba River. Most scholarly accounts of this infamous episode in California history assert that Juanita was the only woman to be lynched during the Gold Rush era. Historians also tell us that the enduring legend of Juanita is due not only to the tragic manner of her death but also to the harsh treatment she received by a bigoted and chauvinistic community based on her ethnicity and gender. The elements of this treatment are symbolic of attitudes toward women and Hispanics that were commonplace throughout the Gold Rush country.

At the time of her death, Juanita was twenty-four years old. Unlike most women who lived in the mining camps, she was not a prostitute. Major Downie, for whom Downieville was later named, wrote, "She was of the Spanish-Mexican mixture, proud and self-possessed, her bearing graceful, almost majestic. She was, in the miner's parlance, 'well put up.'

Juanita was also known for her fiery temper, which was provoked when a miner, Fred Cannon, fell against the door of her house, tearing it from its flimsy hinges. According to witnesses' accounts , Cannon tried to calm Juanita and her live-in boyfriend, Jose, who demanded payment for the damages. Irritated by Jose's demand for money and Juanita's tirade in Spanish, Cannon told Jose to "take [his] whore inside and shut her up."

Screaming that she was not a whore, Juanita reached for a knife and stabbed Cannon in the chest. While Cannon bled to death, a crowd apprehended Jose and Juanita and locked them in a small cabin. Within an hour, a judge and jury of 12 men convened a court and assigned counsel for the defendants. Testimony by several witnesses described Cannon as soft-spoken and not belligerent during the conflict. The same witnesses described Juanita as a firebrand who would not heed Cannon's advice to calm down. After deliberating only 15 minutes, the jury returned a verdict of guilty.

By four o'clock that afternoon, Juanita's lifeless body hung by a rope from the Jersey Bridge. A witness writing for the Pacific Star Newspaper reported that Juanita displayed unusual calm, shook hands with her executioners, and placed the noose around her own neck. Later that night, her body was cut down and delivered into the hands of her friends.

By a strange twist of fate, the murderer and her victim share the same grave. The grave digger, assigned the job of opening graves for both Cannon and Juanita, found the parched ground very hard. To spare himself excessive labor, he created one large grave into which both bodies were placed.

No one knows when Juanita's ghost was first sighted. It is suspected that her spirit was roused in 1870, when the Downieville Cemetery was moved to allow prospectors to hunt for gold. As Juanita's body was moved to another grave, her skull was stolen by members of E Clampus Vitus, a Gold Rush-era fraternal organization with many secret rituals. It is believed that the organization used the skull in its initiation ceremonies, perhaps as a drinking vessel from which new members sipped a secret concoction.

This defamation probably awakened Juanita's spirit and brought her back to the site of her hanging. Several residents of and visitors to Downieville have reported seeing her apparition on the bridge that spans the Yuba River. The current structure was built in 1958, after a flood wiped out the old bridge that served as Juanita's gallows. Nonetheless, the ghost of Juanita walks the bridge and appears to witnesses as a full apparition, a fog in the shape of a human, or a face surrounded by billowing hair. Mary Hansford reported that the apparition appeared to be speaking to her but she heard nothing. I saw the head and torso of Juanita late one moonless night. The apparition moved swiftly from one side of the bridge to the other, crossing the road five times, and then vanished.

GERTRUDE'S GHOST

Downieville River Inn and Resort
121 River Street
Downieville 95936
www.downievilleriverinn.com

The ghost that haunts the popular Downieville River Inn and Resort has a detailed personal history, an unusual occurrence among Gold Rush country legends. Typically, the identity of a ghost is fabricated from conjecture based on a few details and sightings of apparitions that resemble the person depicted in drawings or historic photographs. In the case of this haunted inn, there is no doubt that the busy spirit is that of Era Gertrude Peckwith.

The building now occupied by the inn was built by Gertrude's husband, Ernest, circa 1902. Its construction was supported by gold that Ernest panned in a nearby stream. Little is known of Earnest's later life and death, but it is known that Gertrude was born in 1876 and, at the time of her death, at 5:00 P.M. on August 28, 1958, she weighed 130 pounds and stood 62 inches tall. The spry 82 year old woman was in the habit of taking daily walks around the neighborhood and sometimes wandered to the edge of town to look over the remnants of the Gold Rush days. At 11:00 A.M., on August 27, 1958, while walking across a steep embankment at the Golden Eagle Mine, Gertrude fell, fracturing several ribs and her sternum.

Friends found the elderly lady and carried her to her home, but they failed to appreciate the severity of her injuries and the internal bleeding that resulted from them. Gertrude languished in her house until five o'clock the next evening when she died.

After living in her home for nearly 60 years, Gertrude found it impossible to move on. Her apparition has been seen gliding across the floors of her former bedroom and laundry room. Witnesses told me that she has short gray hair, thin lips, and a pale, translucent face.

Gertrude has been known to climb into bed with guests of the inn or sit on the bed, restraining the movement of their legs. She also changes the temperature of door knobs, making them cold in summer and hot in winter. Ghost hunters who stay in Gertrude's former bedroom should watch the bed for unexplained indentations.

GHOST DANCERS

The Old Masonic Hall
Bigley's Market and Brass Rail
29336 Highway 49
North San Juan 95960-9519
530-292-3095

Constructed in 1853, the old Masonic Hall was the largest building in North San Juan. Money for its construction was donated

The ghosts of miners celebrating their gold discoveries with a dance still haunt the old Masonic Hall in North San Juan.

by local Masons who had become rich, almost overnight, by mining the streams, gullies, and quartz outcroppings in the valley. Having risen meteorically from the lowly station of starving, rag-clad miners to that of prominent, wealthy citizens in the inner sanctum of the secret society of Freemasonry, the men created an edifice that not only concealed their secret rituals from outsiders but also stood as a monument to their great accomplishments. During its first 40 years, the great hall was well-kept, with ornate furnishings, a long, well-stocked bar, and fancy wall and window coverings. Late in the 1890s, after local gold mining operations ceased, the town's population fell to less than 100 people, leaving only a few Masons to carry on their traditions and maintain the building.

By 1920, the old building had lost its charm. The first floor was leased to two businessmen, who opened a general store and post office, while the second floor was used as a boarding house. In the late 1920s and early 1930s, my mother spent most of her summers in North San Juan. She recalls that the general store was the only place in town where ice could be found. Today, the first floor is divided between a grocery store and the Brass Rail, a popular bar.

The second floor of the old hall is used for storage of nonperishable food and liquor. A young lady who works in the grocery store told me that employees go upstairs only once or twice each week, yet the sound of heavy boots walking across the floor is heard daily. These strange sounds have been noted when witnesses are certain no one has entered the second floor. The sound of shoes shuffling across the floor is also heard, usually in the evening. One witness said he thought he heard sounds of several people dancing upstairs. These ghostly feet moved in unison, as though they were keeping time with music only they could hear. During my last visit to North San Juan I requested permission to do an EVP sweep upstairs. This request was denied since the owner was not in town and could not be reached. I was told, however, that most of the town's residents know about the ghostly dancers in the Masonic Hall. In fact, ghostly images of miners, pioneers, travelers, and other characters from the 1860s are often seen in the narrow streets of this town.

GHOST OF THE CHURCH PEOPLE

United Methodist Church
Flume Street, North San Juan 95960
530-289-3140

Perched on a little hill overlooking a cluster of aged buildings that once comprised the heart of North San Juan's business district, the United Methodist Church was once a beacon of salvation for the decent citizens of this wild mining town. Founded in 1853 by a German miner named Christian Kientz, the town's population jumped from less than 50 to nearly 5,000 as better mining techniques uncovered greater riches and complex water flumes brought much-needed water to operate machinery.

By 1856, respectable citizens established public services such as a school, city hall, marshal's office and jail, and the little church on Flume Street. They commissioned the Reverend H. B. Sheldon to include North San Juan in his circuit, which included French

Ghosts of church people still show up for services in North San Juan.

Corral, Brandy City, and a couple of camps whose names are lost to history. The good reverend rode horseback from town to town, holding services, performing baptisms, and presiding over funerals. The building is still in use as a Methodist church, with Sunday services and a Sunday school.

The interior of this aged building has been restored and appears as it did in the 1850s. On the hand-hewn floorboards and pews, visitors can see the marks left by Gold Rush era craftsman who worked without power tools. Outside, the heavy beams that support the structure also show the marks of axe and adz. Sturdy construction and a lucky location spared the church from destruction in the 1860s and 1870s, when three major fires wiped out the business district.

Each time I have sat alone in a pew, the distinct sounds of church people fade in and continue for a few minutes before fading away. These sounds include hushed conversations, the swishing of long skirts in motion, shuffling of boots on the wood floors, soft footsteps, and the creaking of the wooden pews as invisible parishioners sit down. I have never captured these sounds on tape, but amorphous light anomalies appear in some of my digital pictures. I've also felt the passage of invisible people as they moved down the pew past me. This sensation includes a thickened atmosphere and temperature drop.

With a history that spans more than 150 years of weddings, funerals, baptisms, and worship services during stressful times brought by wars, the Depression, and natural disasters, the emotional energy expended in this little building must have been intense. To me, the place feels crowded with the spirit remnants of parishioners but there may be a real ghost here, too. A resident of North San Juan told me that the apparition of a tall man dressed in black sometimes appears near the front door of the church. This may be the Reverend H. B. Sheldon, still riding his circuit through the Gold Rush country.

GHOST OF THE GRAVE DIGGER

North San Juan Protestant Cemetery
End of Cemetery Lane
North San Juan 95860

This fascinating cemetery can be seen from Highway 49, if you know where to look. The thick canopy of trees and layers of dust, dirt, and moss on headstones conspire to conceal the monuments from people passing through the little hamlet of North San Juan. The sign marking Cemetery Lane can be difficult to spot, too. Look for Bigley's Market and the Brass Rail Bar; Cemetery Lane will be across the street.

Opened a few months after the town was founded in 1853, the cemetery sits on a hill that pioneers stripped of trees for firewood and building materials. This defoliation afforded the dearly departed a nice view of the town, while the tall, granite monuments offered a sobering reminder to drunk miners and outlaws passing through town that life is short.

There are recent graves in this cemetery, and ghost hunters should respect these and their visitors. Most of the graves, however, date from the Gold Rush era, including those of many children. I found several graves of people who were born in Europe and in the eastern United States in the 1790s. The early dates of birth indicate that these people embarked on a land or sea journey to the Gold Rush country at relatively old ages, arriving in the 1850s. The headstones of these graves indicate that the latest date of death among this generation was 1866.

Today, the dense overhead canopy and tall shrubs block out intrusions of the twenty-first century, including motorcycles on nearby Highway 49, and create a spooky ambience even at midday. Long shadows create the perfect atmosphere for the ghost of a gravedigger to appear. This fellow is short and hunched over, as if he is carrying a heavy load on his back. His only visible load, however, is a long-handled shovel resting on his shoulder. The man's clothing looks dirty and ragged, and he wears a straw hat.

This ghost can be seen in the shadows, but he vanishes when he moves through shafts of sunlight that penetrate the trees. I have watched this fellow for as long as thirty seconds as he floats across the graveyard, sometimes passing through monuments. He appears to float because his lower legs and feet are invisible. I made audio recordings in this graveyard that produced the sounds of a flute, which may be a remnant of music played as part of a graveside service, or else one of the graveyard's residents may have been a musician.

GHOST OF THE SQUIRE and THE LADY IN GRAY

109 Prospect Street
Nevada City 95959
530-265-5135
www.redcastleinn.com

Standing to the east of Highway 49, a short distance from the once wild Gold Rush town of Nevada City, is a magnificent brick mansion known as the Red Castle. The stately old place stands amid a thick grove of trees on a hillside, giving the appearance of standing away from the quaint town with its rush of tourists and modernity. Today, the Red Castle is a popular bed and breakfast inn that hosts many visitors who come to see some of the most active ghosts of the Gold Rush era.

The four-story mansion was built in 1860 by John Williams, a businessman from Illinois who made a small fortune in the gold fields (which is used interchangeably with the terms "diggings" and "gold

The ghosts of Squire John Williams and the Lady in Gray haunt this brick mansion in Nevada City.

mines"). His success, education, and popularity in the Deer Creek mining camp (which would later become Nevada City) resulted in his election as Justice of the Peace and the title Squire Williams. His large family, including his wife, Abigail, his children, and many foster children, enjoyed the spacious home for many years until John's death on February 8, 1871. John's son, Loring, stepped in as patriarch of the family, but he died three years later, also in February. Loring's will directed that his funeral be held at the same time and on the same day of the week as his father's funeral. Both somber events took place in the living room of the Red Castle. With the men of the house gone, Loring's wife, Cornelia, and mother, Abigail, were left to carry on, supported only by a capable and reliable nanny, known today as the Lady in Gray.

When the frail Cornelia died June 18, 1883, Abigail faced the greatest challenges of her life. She struggled to keep the mansion and the family's financial affairs in order, but eventually exhausted her husband's fortune. She sold the mansion in 1891 and moved to southern California. The children moved away to various cities.

Throughout the 1870s and 1880s, the many children and foster children housed on the topmost floor of the Red Castle were under the supervision of a governess. Her name is unknown, but ghost hunters call her the Lady in Gray. Her ghost and the ghost of Squire John Williams are often sighted moving about the mansion. The ghost of Cornelia Williams, whose funeral was held in the parlor in 1883, is also seen as a pale, partial apparition. Her full skirt is seen and heard as she moves about the parlor or leaves the room through the pocket doors.

John Williams' ghost appears as an old, bearded man dressed in a black frock coat and, sometimes, a tall hat. He has appeared throughout the house at various times during renovations as if to inspect the work being done. His life-like apparition was seen in such detail by workmen that they assumed he was a local character who wandered into the mansion out of curiosity. When the specter vanished before their eyes, workers decided it had been the ghost of the Squire watching over his house. Guests of the inn have spotted this ghost on the veranda when it was covered with snow, but when staff investigated the sighting no footprints were found.

The most active ghost in the Red Castle is the Lady in Gray, so named because she wears a gray Victorian gown. Many visitors to the inn have encountered this ghost and thought she was a staff member in period costume. She has entered guest rooms and carried on conversations, talking about the children under her care. This ghost has been seen with a small dog in her arms walking halls of the house, and has appeared in every room on the fourth floor.

I have visited several times, always staying in a room on the fourth floor. During each visit, I heard the sounds of children laughing and talking. The first time I entered a room on this floor with my wife, I distinctly heard a young girl say, "There're going into our room." I've witnessed the apparitions of John Williams, the Lady in Gray, and a tall, hooded figure on the main floor. Other ghostly activity at this inn includes a strange light that appears around the beds, cold spots, and great EVP.

MUSEUM GHOSTS

Nevada County Historical Museum
Firehouse No. 1
215 Main Street
Nevada City 95959-2509
530-265-5468
www.nevadacountyhistory.org

Like most ramshackle towns of the Gold Rush era, in its early days as a mining camp Nevada City was prone to fires among the dry, wooden shacks servicing the somewhat transient population. The risk and fear of fire was so great that the town's female citizens went door to door and scraped up the funds for the construction of two firehouses. Firehouse No. 1 was built at the lower end of the business district, while Firehouse No. 2 was placed on Broad Street near the homes of the town's wealthiest citizens. Although the two facilities were constructed at the same time, their designs are completely different. Firehouse No. 1 is an aging yet beautiful structure of brick and wood, with a bell tower and Victorian-style gingerbread trim. Today, it houses the Nevada County Historical Museum, which features artifacts from the ill-fated Donner party, the city's earliest Chinese residents, and houses of ill-repute. Many of these historic objects came to the museum with a ghost attached.

Several ghosts began making appearances on the second and third floors of the firehouse soon after Gold Rush-era photographs, furniture, and other historical items were moved into the building. Among the most frequently sighted apparitions is that of a red-haired woman frequently described as looking like she worked in a bordello who sits at the old piano. The piano was donated to the museum after standing for many years in a house of ill-repute in Auburn. This ghost does not play music, but she appears life-like and makes eye contact with people who show an interest in the piano.

Nevada City's Firehouse No. 1 is now a historical museum with Gold Rush-era antiques and several ghosts.

The spirit of another woman appears close to the hutch and rocking chair on display o the second floor. Dressed in a Victorian gown, this ghost has been seen searching the various compartments of the hutch.

The red-haired woman also sometimes leaves her piano to sit in the rocking chair and look through the hutch.

The extraordinary picture of Mr. Carrigan hangs on the second floor inside a glass case. The photograph was taken when Carrigan was about fifty years old. It is said that when the photograph was taken he was thinking about his childhood. When the photograph was developed a second image appeared, that of Carrigan as a boy.

On the ground floor of the museum stands a thousand-year-old Taoist shrine believed to be the oldest in North America. People who stand in front of the shrine have felt unseen hands try to push them aside, and passersby often feel tripped up. Some visitors have reported seeing several Chinese men loitering in front of the shrine, kneeling, pacing, or standing with bowed heads, as though praying. Chants have been picked up on audio recorders, and EVP often consist of voices speaking Chinese.

THE SHOW NEVER ENDS

Nevada Theatre
401 Broad Street
Nevada City 95959
530-265-6161

From the ghost hunter's perspective, theatres are like ships—all of them are haunted. In the case of century-old music halls, silent movie theatres, vaudeville auditoriums, opera houses, and grand playhouses, so much energy was expended by passionate actors, musicians, choreographers, and directors that it would be surprising not to find environmental imprints or spirit remnants. Ghosts are common in these places, too. I've investigated many theatres where stagehands died of accidents such as falling off catwalks high above the stage or being crushed by collapsing scenery. Some stage hands committed suicide when they realized the beautiful star they loved would never get involved with a working man. The ghosts of anxiety-ridden stars who could not face the inevitable decline of their careers often haunt theatres where they experienced their greatest success. At Le Petit Theatre du Vieux Carre, in New Orleans, I once encountered the ghost of an actress killed by a jealous rival.

The Nevada Theatre is haunted by the ghosts of a man and a woman. Several groups of paranormal investigators have visited this place over the past ten years, but none of them have been able to identify the ghosts haunting this historic building. Opened September 9, 1865, the building hardly looks its age. It resembles a concrete box of the warehouse variety. But inside, visitors detect the ambience of the 19th century and architectural features from the Gold Rush-era. Its wide stage once served as a platform for performers such as Emma Nevada, Mark Twain, Lotta Crabtree, and Edwin Booth, brother of the Lincoln assassin. Since its inception nearly 150 years ago, the theater has remained in continuous use as an entertainment venue, barring an 11 year period that ended in 1968. After this period of inactivity and renovation, at least the two aforementioned ghosts became active.

The ghosts spotted in the Nevada Theatre are believed to be performers. They are stylishly dressed in early 20th century clothing, complete with hats. It is likely that they were vaudeville performers who traveled from town to town, putting on the same show for a few days before moving on. I was unable to uncover any records of accidents, natural deaths, or other events that might have led to this double haunting. It is possible that these two ghosts loved this particular theatre, the town, or the adoring audience so much that they decided to stay.

My first visit to the Nevada Theatre was not intended as a ghost hunt, but I witnessed this couple float down the aisle moments before the production got underway. The audience had been seated and quieted by dimmed lights, but before the music started this ghostly couple passed from the rear of the theatre toward the stage. Before reaching the stage, they vanished. They looked so real, I thought they were part of the show. They smiled and appeared to be looking over the audience, thrilled that the house was packed. Expressions on the faces of people around me registered no surprise, so I assumed they had not noticed the ghostly couple.

The best way for ghost hunters to have a fulfilling experience with the paranormal in this place is to attend a performance. Meet one of the producers, directors, or stage managers and make arrangements for an after-hours visit. Visiting the restroom might also be productive from a paranormal perspective. Gold Rush-era figures have appeared in the mirrors in both the men's and women's restrooms.

GHOSTS OF THE POWER BROKERS

National Hotel
211 Broad Street
Nevada City 95959
530-265-4551
www.thenationalhotel.com

The National Hotel is the largest building on Nevada City's historic Broad Street. Constructed in the mid-1850s by enlarging and joining together three existing structures, it opened as the luxurious National Exchange Hotel on August 20, 1856. Its spacious dining room, bar, and second floor lobby have retained all the charm of the great Gold Rush boom years, when lucky miners paid for extravagant meals and a few nights in a feather bed by dropping a leather pouch filled with gold nuggets on the clerk's desk. The hotel also attracted well-heeled mining engineers from as far away as England and investment bankers from San Francisco.

In 1905, the second floor lobby was used as a meeting place by the power brokers who founded California's largest energy company, Pacific Gas and Electric, Incorporated. PG & G continues to supply the northern half of the state with energy, but few of its millions of customers realize the company got its humble start in this Gold Rush town.

The lobby used for this auspicious event is located on the second floor of the hotel, overlooking the street. Many guests have walked through the lobby late at night and noticed several men dressed in Victorian-era suits, sitting in the antique chairs and smoking cigars. Their clothing might not be such a surprise, because at various times of the year townspeople and visitors wearing period costumes crowd the streets and fill the hotels in celebration of California's statehood, the Fourth of July, or Christmas. But the cigars and vacant expressions of these stoic fellows clearly gives the impression that they are not living in the present. Finally, their cigars leave no trace of smoke in the air, yet the odor is unmistakable. Since smoking is not allowed in the hotel and these fellows appear transparent, witnesses are thrilled to have seen this amazing gathering of ghosts.

In the same room, a box piano sits next to a wall. This antique

The National Hotel in Nevada City has been accumulating ghosts since 1856.

was built on the East Coast and shipped around Cape Horn to San Francisco, then carried over land by wagon to be placed in the hotel around 1858. The piano cannot be played, yet its melodic notes are often heard late at night. This would be a good location for ghost hunters to perform an EVP sweep.

I have stayed in the National Hotel a total of more than seven nights and always experienced something paranormal. My first night, while sleeping alone, I heard the door to my room open and close more than twenty times over a four hours period. A housekeeper told me that the occupants of many of the rooms report the sound of the door opening and closing even when the deadbolt is set.

I've felt an invisible person sit on my bed while I lay reading with the lights on, encountered icy cold spots, heard someone humming in my ear while I tried to fall asleep, and walked into a patch of thick air that left me feeling nauseated.

During my last visit to the National Hotel, the bartender told me about the most recent paranormal activity noticed in the bar. Late at night, while preparing to close the bar, staff members have noticed the strong odor of cigar smoke. The odor persists in all areas of the bar until the last staff member touches the door knob on leaving. At that instant, the odor is suddenly gone. It is as if ghostly late-night customers enjoy a smoke as they watch the friendly staff close up, then the ghosts extinguish their smokes and go home.

In several areas of the bar, banging sounds have been heard emanating from the walls. Plumbers have not discovered loose pipes or structural anomalies that could account for these persistently loud sounds. A more frightening sound moves from one spot to another, making late-night staff nervous about being in the bar alone. This sound was described to me as that of a screeching cat, or two cats involved in a fight. The sound does not come from under the floor or outside the hotel. Witnesses are certain it arises from unseen beings inside the bar itself. When the screeching reaches its greatest intensity it moves from one side of the barroom to the other, away from curious witnesses who approach. One staff member told me it does not sound like two cats but two women engaged in a vicious fight. Given the notorious history of the bar, this may be an auditory remnant of a "cat fight" that took place in the mid-1800s.

EDGAR AND A FULL HOUSE

Holbrooke Hotel
212 West Main Street
Grass Valley 95945
916-273-1353
www.Holbrookeehotel.net/history/

Ghost hunters who visit the beautiful and historic Holbrooke Hotel may encounter something more than ghosts. At times, the place is crawling with paranormal investigators. On several occasions, I have turned down a darkened hallway only to find several people standing in a guestroom, staring at the walls or listening for disembodied sounds. To many observers this might appear to be strange behavior, but when I see people snapping pictures of walls, waving sensing devices around, and speaking into audio recorders it is clear that they are ghost hunters. During my last visit to the Holbrooke Hotel, I encountered a dozen members of HPI, a Sacramento-based group.

The Holbrooke Hotel in Grass Valley has been investigated by several ghost hunters, who always capture orbs or fascinating EVP.

The Holbrooke Hotel has the kind of history that arouses the interest of ghost hunters. Its location in a Gold Rush town is of paramount importance, but the development of the property since 1852, its colorful owners and patrons, and threats from fire create all the ingredients required for attracting ghosts. The beauty of the place and 19th-century ambience may be the reason many ghosts remain there.

The original structure at the site was the Golden Gate Saloon. Opened in the summer of 1852, this landmark bar was popular with miners who struck it rich in nearby creeks. By 1853, a single-story hotel was added to the rear of the saloon. It was known as the Exchange Hotel in recognition of the exchange of gold dust and nuggets for coin that took place in the adjoining saloon.

The saloon was destroyed in the great fire of 1855 and rebuilt with fieldstone and brick. As wealth from nearby hard-rock mines poured into Grass Valley, the saloon and hotel were renovated and absorbed into a much larger structure that still stands today. The new hotel offered spacious and luxurious rooms, a large bar, and the best restaurant in the region. Named in 1879 for owner D. P. Holbrooke, the hotel attracted wealthy mining engineers, actresses like Lola Montez and Lotta Crabtree, writers such as Mark Twain, Bret Harte, and Jack London, and ex-presidents including Ulysses S. Grant, James Garfield, and Benjamin Harrison. The fancy hotel also attracted gamblers, pickpockets, thieves, and prostitutes.

Today, the hotel is popular among the living and spirits alike. Members of HPI shared with me some of their photos of orbs, which seemed to be found in every guestroom they visited. In a room named for Benjamin Harrison I caught a few orbs in my photos. This is indicative of intense spirit activity, as I rarely capture orbsin areas with low-level activity. aSpirits in the Lotta Crabtree room generated orbs on every camera used, along with some interesting EVP.

Four apparitions have been seen in several locations in the Holbrooke Hotel. A female ghost with long, blonde hair wearing mid-17th century attire walks the hallways of the second floor. Some witnesses have followed her as she walked more than 50 feet before she vanished or passed through a closed door into a guestroom. Some guests and ghost hunters have reported encounters with this ghost that do not include visual phenomena. They report the scent of perfume, the sound of a long dress swishing as the lady walks, and other impressions that make them feel as though they are being watched or touched lightly. Those who felt the touch of this ghost reported that the sensation made the hair on their arms stand on end.

In the basement, the Iron Door restaurant is haunted by the ghost of a man dressed as a cowboy. This spirit is likely that of a man who died within the past 50 years, because his outfit does not resemble clothing worn by 19th century cowboys. This ghostly fellow is decked out in a striped shirt, a white hat, tight-fitting pants, and boots with spurs. Witnesses report that this man appears for a few seconds leaning against a post in the dining room, then vanishes. There is no historical information or psychic communication that gives clues as to the identity of this ghost or why he is here.

The ghost of a little girl named Elizabeth has been spotted by several children. Many who are frightened by Elizabeth's sudden appearance and disappearance run crying to their parents, screaming that they've seen a ghost. It is believed that Elizabeth died in the hotel early in the 20th century. In addition to this apparition, the disembodied sound of children playing has been heard at several locations within the hotel.

A former manager of the hotel haunts the bar and lobby. Known as Edgar the Ghost, this apparition shows up when there are a lot of people around. It is said that he got into some kind of trouble at the hotel, perhaps during its Speak Easy days during Prohibition. Edgar may be responsible for TVs turning on and off, light flickering, and doors slamming.

Other places at the Holbrooke Hotel where visitors may encounter ghosts include the women's restroom in the basement; room one, where guests have heard the sound of chains hitting the wall or their name called, and experienced strange forces; and rooms 14 and 15, where gold dust and bullion were once counted and stored.

THREE NUNS

Mount St. Mary's Convent and Academy
410 South Church Street
Grass Valley 95945
530-273-5509

When I first visited this historic building, I hoped I would encounter paranormal remnants of my grandmother. I didn't expect to find her

Mount St. Mary's Convent in Grass Valley was home for my grandmother while her father dashed off to the Alaska Gold Rush. Her spirit rests elsewhere, but several other ghosts do haunt this building.

ghost, but I wondered if she might have left an environmental imprint on the third floor. In 1904, my grandmother, Harriet Stevenson, and her brother, Arthur, were left in the care of the good sisters of St. Mary's Convent and Orphan Asylum by their father, Arthur Sr. The mother of the children was dying of typhoid and could no longer care for them. Arthur Sr. had few prospects for ensuring the future security of little Harriet and Arthur Jr. until an opportunity came his way to join a gold prospecting expedition in Alaska.

Arthur Sr. spent nearly three years in Alaska making his fortune. When he returned to Grass Valley, he recovered his children and moved to Seattle, where he built a fine house. Later, the family moved to Oakland, California.

I remember my grandmother telling me how sad she was as she watched her mother die and her father depart for a far away land she knew nothing about. She also told me stories about the orphanage, including the strict nuns, the regimen of daily life, and hard work making beds and washing the floor in the children's dormitory. Working for hours on her hands and knees, scrubbing the floor was the hardest work she ever did. When I walked that floor, I looked an every scratch and groove, wondering if my grandmother had touched them.

During many visits to this convent over a period of 20 years, I never saw the apparition of a little girl, but I saw other remnants of the nuns and residents who lived and worked there in the late 19th and early 20th centuries. Several times I saw the partial apparition of three nuns, visible from the waist up, walk together across the second and third floors. Their faces were obscured by headscarves, but their black and white garments were unmistakable. On the third floor, where the children's dormitories were, I detected the laughter and sobbing of children. Others have reported the disembodied sounds of several feet racing across the floor as though on their way to school.

Ghost hunters who visit this place may encounter paranormal activity, including EVP and orbs, at any location. The entire building is imprinted with intense emotions of orphans and other children who were given up by families unable to care for them. The first orphans were taken in on March 20, 1866. A few days later, more orphans arrived, described as "four of the most miserable creatures, blind, lame, and poverty stricken in the extreme." When the orphanage closed in 1932, its roll of child residents included over a thousand names. The intense emotions of these destitute children have left this building full of imprints that may be detected by sensitive ghost hunters.

GHOST OF THE GRAVE GUARDIANS

St. Patrick's Catholic Cemetery
South Church at Chapel Street
Grass Valley 95945
530-271-5947

This eerie cemetery sits across the street from St. Mary's Convent and St. Patrick's Church. In spite of the local traffic of church-goers and tourists, the cemetery looks neglected. Tall weeds gather near the trees and, in some cases, adorn graves. Many of the grave markers are broken, wrought iron fences are disjointed and rusted, and some of the concrete borders and grave covers are cracked. This state of neglect may be attributed to the fact that descendants of the deceased no longer live nearby. The cemetery opened in 1853 and several generations have passed since the first burials. Some headstones are so badly weathered or damaged by vandals that the names of the grave's occupants cannot be read. All of this gives the graveyard a particularly macabre atmosphere, especially at night. Aside from the uneven ground and hazards that may be concealed by tall grass or weeds, this graveyard is relatively safe for ghost hunters who visit at night.

Many professional ghost hunters, including myself, agree that ghosts do not generally haunt a graveyard because they have nowhere better to go. Ghosts who remain in a graveyard are there because they are disturbed by the condition of their graves. They may want to draw the attention of the living to make repairs, clean the headstone, remove garbage, or secure the coffin.

During my visits to St. Patrick's Cemetery, I discovered ghostly activity at two locations where the graves were badly damaged. Edward Corbett died at the age of 38 years on November 23, 1866. His elaborate grave is enclosed by a short wall composed of bricks. The decay of mortar has allowed many of these bricks to fall out of place, giving the grave the appearance that it is slowly collapsing. At night, an unseen entity walks the perimeter of this grave, always in a counter-clockwise direction. Sensitive ghost hunters will hear the sound of boots on the grass. If you stand in one spot next to the wall, you may feel a cold, thick atmosphere engulf you every minute. I have stood at this grave and felt this odd sensation, accompanied by brief nausea, every minute for more than ten minutes before it fades away.

At the north end of the graveyard, the once elegant headstone of John Judd stands broken and badly weathered. John died at the age of 39 years on November 3, 1860. He probably spent his last years mourning for his daughter, Marie, who died October 18, 1858 at the age of seven. Sadly, another daughter, seven-month-old Mary, died soon after John, on March 21, 1861. All three occupy this grave, but John is not at rest. The sound of a man sobbing can be heard in the evening. The ghost that creates this sound also generates an atmosphere of profound sadness. A colleague of mine who is a psychic sensed that John is angry that the monument has been damaged because he wants his daughters to have a beautiful grave. Some ghost hunters have obtained EVP at this site that sound like a man crying.

GHOST OF THE SCREAMING LADY

Empire Mine
10791 Empire Street
Grass Valley
530-273-8522
www.ncgold.com/history/EmpireMine/history.html

From George Roberts' discovery of a gold-laden quartz outcropping in 1850 to the Empire Mine's closure in 1956, nearly six million ounces of gold were extracted from 367 miles of underground passages. Over the course of a century, disasters such as cave-ins, fires, and flooding took their toll on miners while the fluctuating value of gold sometimes brought engineers and owners to the brink of financial disaster. The lives lost and fortunes gained may account for the many ghosts that haunt this lavish estate and mining facility that stands today as a monument to California's hard rock gold miners, engineers, and entrepreneurs.

Ghosts of men who died in the Empire Mine may haunt the Grass Valley mansion of mine owner William Bourne.

By 1870, Empire Mine owner William Bourn Sr. had created a state-of-the-art mining operation that employed experienced miners form Cornwall, England. The most advanced equipment was installed, including Cornish pumps which increased productivity by draining water from flooded shafts. In 1877, William Bourn Jr. inherited the mine from his father and continued the tradition of utilizing the most modern technology. Using stone extracted from the mine, Bourn built a mansion on the property that was the finest in the region. Interior walls of redwood, leaded-glass windows, and beautiful gardens were created without care for expense, yet the place was referred to as "the cottage." Bourn Jr. spent more money on his even larger estate, Filoli, located 20 miles south of San Francisco, but he was so attached to the cottage that his ghost often shows up there. Docents who work in the mansion admit they often feel the presence of William Bourn as he looks over the place, as if to ensure that nothing has changed since the late 1800s. Creaking floorboards are heard when no one is moving about and isolated cold drafts give the impression that something paranormal is occurring.

The image of a woman dressed in Edwardian-era clothing has been seen by docents and visitors and captured in photographs. Her mouth is open wide, as if she is screaming, but no sound is detected. The image of an older woman, dressed elegantly in an Edwardian gown, has been discovered in photographs taken in the main floor living room. This ghost is believed to be the wife of William Bourn, Sr.

In the entrance to the mineshaft, sensitive visitors may hear the hushed voices of miners and engineers as they prepare to ride the elevators that took them deep underground. The sound of machinery also may be heard. Photographs and digital images taken here often exhibit orbs.

Other places to look for ghosts:

CONSTABLE JACK'S

515 Main Street
Newcastle 95658
916-663-9385
www.constablejacks.com

Named for the constable of old Auburn, this popular blues nightclub and restaurant was declared haunted by Shannon McCabe, president of HPI. The ghost of a young man named Gary causes glasses and wine bottles to fly off the shelves. A young female ghost named Emily is also seen here. She has long, blonde hair and wears a long dress. The ghost hunters of HPI picked up some good EVP here. A female voice said "Help me," while a male voice said "get out" and "we are dead."

PLACER COUNTY COURTHOUSE

101 Maple Street at Lincoln Way
Auburn 95603
530-887-2111

This prominent, spooky building can be seen from the freeway. It often attracts the attention of passersby, who can't resist stopping for a closer look at the place. Built in 1898 of locally quarried stone, the structure once housed the county jail and sheriff's office on the first floor, where ghosts of prisoners who died in their cells still roam. Nearly 40 years before the courthouse's construction, the site was used for public hangings and bullfights. Sensitive visitors may hear the sound of cell doors swinging on rusty hinges.

LOLA MONTEZ HOME

248 Mill Street
Grass Valley 95945

Irish-born Lola Montez (1821-1861) arrived in Grass Valley in July of 1853 after a scandalous decade in Europe as a Spanish dancer and consort to King Ludwig I of Bavaria. Her famous spider dance and liberated attitudes made her an instant hit with miners. In spite of her fame, she lived in a modest home that now houses the Chamber of Commerce. Much of this building has been rebuilt over the past 160 years, but the door and its fixtures are original. The mechanical door buzzer—activated by a clockwise motion of the key—has been known to sound without a visible, living being at the door. The doorknob turns and rattles as if someone is trying to get inside. Whether these frequent and bizarre occurrences are the handiwork of Lola Montez or others who lived in the house remains unknown.

U.S. HOTEL

233 B Broad Street
Nevada City 95959
530-265-7999

This once-popular hotel was closed in 2008, but local ghost hunters believe the spirit of Robber Baron Charles Crocker still haunts the place. When guests stayed in Crocker's favorite room, they complained to the manager of a strong odor of cigar smoke. Since smoking is forbidden anywhere in the building, the only logical explanation is paranormal. When the hotel re-opens in 2009, it will be a good venue for ghost hunters. Long periods of vacancy followed by renovation or remodeling tend to rouse spirits.

HARDSCRAPPLE BUILDING

107 West Main street
Nevada City 95959

This two-story brick building was constructed in 1852 and re-constructed a few years later. In the 19th century, it served several merchants, including a furniture seller and an undertaker. Today, a law office is housed on the second floor while a consignment-clothing store occupies the space formerly used as a mortuary. A stone wall that stands two-stories high may be linked to paranormal activity noted in the building. The mineral content of the stones may create the perfect electromagnetic environment for hauntings.

L GRILL AND SALOON

134 Mill Street
Grass Valley 95945

A ghost named George haunts this old west drinking and eating establishment. It has been reported that George was caught cheating at poker and shot in or near booth number seven. George causes barroom doors to swing rhythmically for minutes without slowing, items to fly off the shelves of the back bar, and shot glasses to slide on the tables. Some staff members believe an unexplained shadow is George's apparition.

CHAPTER 4

The North-Central Gold Diggings: From Auburn to Diamond Springs

Soon after the discovery of gold at Coloma in 1848, several camps and towns sprang up on nearby creeks and tributaries of the American River, populated by 49ers who panned the frigid waters for the precious metal. Some towns, such as Georgetown, were remote, perched on high plateaus of the Sierra Nevada over quartz outcroppings where California's great gold mines would later be dug. Others, like Auburn and Placerville, were founded along the heavily traveled routes from Sacramento to the diggings of the central Sierra. Today, these towns flourish on business derived from travelers on busy Interstate 80 and Highway 50, but they retain their Gold Rush-era appearance through preserved buildings now used for stores, inns, restaurants, and bars.

Most of the towns of this region endured long periods of lawlessness as gold seekers, saloon keepers, gamblers, con men, and bandits rushed into the area intent on quick riches, legal or otherwise. In old Dry Diggings, the townspeople took justice into their own hands several times. By 1852, so many outlaws had been hanged that the town became known as Hangtown. By 1855, law and order was established, and the town was renamed Placerville after a development in mining techniques that flushed more gold from the hillsides.

GRAVEYARD GHOSTS

Greenwood Pioneer Cemetery
Greenwood Road
Greenwood 95635

With the exception of a few graves decorated with plastic flowers and remnants of visits made long ago, this pioneer cemetery appears neglected. Several broken and toppled headstones remain as monuments to the rough passage of 150 years and the destruction wreaked by vandals. The graveyard sits on the west side of Greenwood Road behind a wire fence that stands about four feet high. Sweeping upward from the road, the cemetery has an eerie atmosphere even in broad daylight. The first grave established here was for William Leed of Lawrenceburg. A veteran of the Mexican War and native of Indiana, this gentleman died after finding gold in the creek that runs through the center of town.

A once-thriving gold rush town with many rich mines and a legitimate aspiration to become the county seat, Greenwood is now more of a ghost town than a town of the living. I managed to find two lively local residents, however, who told me about the well-publicized experiences of young people in the cemetery. Out for a night of thrills and fun, these kids encountered the frightening presence of a tall man strong enough to push the intruders around. Psychic and ghost hunter Nancy Bradley wrote about an encounter such as this in her book. I learned that the phantom still haunts the old graveyard, moaning, walking about, and brushing against visitors.

Years ago, psychic Sharon Turner once visited this graveyard with Nancy Bradley. They discovered a male ghost here who is searching for someone named Lana. His appearance and demeanor matched the reports of local children. Historic records indicate that a child named Alana died in Greenwood at the age of three months. The child's father preceded her in death by two months.

My visits to the graveyard have been made during the day, but dark, overcast skies created an atmosphere that felt electrically charged. I saw an apparition that consisted of an upper torso, two arms, and a head nearly covered with long hair and a beard. Clearly a man, the expression on this apparition's face was of pain and frustration. He moved quickly past several headstones, gazing at them as if he was trying to read the inscriptions. If this is the same ghost that Bradley described, he may be looking for the grave of baby Alana.

When standing next to some of the broken headstones, I detected very faint moaning and mumbling, and the occasional light touch of weak hands on my back. Noted ghost hunter and writer Troy Taylor suggests that most graveyard ghosts haunt their burial sites only when monuments are vandalized or broken by natural elements. These spirits are trying to get the attention of the living with the hope that repairs would be made to their final resting place.

PHANTOMS GATHERED AT THE HANGING TREE

The Ricci Building
Greenwood Road
Greenwood 95635

Founded in 1848, Greenwood was once a thriving town that rode the waves of riches that came first from nearby creeks, then from the mines. Looking at the town today, though, it is nearly to impossible to imagine that this tiny village was once an important town with a sawmill, two theatres, a Wells Fargo office, a stage-coach service, a large hotel, several boarding houses, 14 general stores, two breweries, and an unknown number of private residences. Today, only a few buildings that were standing during the 1860s remain on the town's main street, Greenwood Road. The brick Ricci building, constructed in 1920, is an exact replica of the original that stood on the site and burned to the ground in 1912. Many businesses thrived at this location, including a mortuary. I spoke to two residents who told me about ghostly images of Gold Rush people who roam the main street as if they were still alive.

The apparitions of a woman and her young son are frequently seen near the hanging tree, which stands near the Ricci building. The ghost of a town drunk has been spotted staggering down the street with a bottle in his hand. A miner named Duke gives the impression that he is happy about something, perhaps the discovery of a rich gold mine. One of the most frequently seen ghosts is that of a tall, slim man dressed in black pants and vest and a white shirt. Witnesses describe him as a lawyer or merchant. One resident told me she thought this was the ghost of Justice of the Peace Sam Crane.

Among Greenwood's civic institutions was a circuit court presided over by Judge Lynch and law enforcement administered by Sheriff Tom Birch and Justice of the Peace Sam Crane. On several occasions, these men captured and tried murderers, condemning them to death. The town's official hanging tree still stands near the Ricci building, and the ghosts of the men who died at this spot, more than 150 years ago, still create intense paranormal activity.

According to a history of Greenwood written in 1883, the first to die on the town's hanging tree was James Graham. Caught in nearby Uniontown, Graham was returned to Greenwood by Sheriff Birch, then tried and hung in less than an hour. On July 23, 1854, Samuel Allen swung from a rope after a crowd of angry citizens removed him from the sheriff's custody. Allen's crime was particularly heinous; he killed the elderly William Shay and then repeatedly smashed the victim's head with a stone "crushing it to jelly."

In August of 1857, Henry Miller murdered Harrison Hilton after a dispute about the use of water in a creek. On September 1, a committee drafted a lengthy document that recognized the high moral character, citizenship, and honest enterprise of the victim. With that bit of business completed, members of the committee then hanged Miller from the oak tree. The drop from a toppled stool nearly decapitated the prisoner. According to witness accounts, when his corpse was cut down his head was separated from his body by prodding from a pitchfork.

The ghosts of these murderers are believed to be attached to the old hanging tree and visible to sensitive ghost hunters. Most of these spirits are seen standing near the tree, but one fellow hangs at the end of a rope. Psychic Sharon Turner suggests that this man was innocent and cannot get past the event of his death because he will not release his claim of innocence.

Residual hauntings or imprints created by the emotions of townspeople who beheld the hangings may also be detected. Writer and psychic Nancy Bradley reported that people have heard the ghost of a woman, standing at the hanging tree, explain to her ghost son that the men who were executed at the site "were not godly." If this report is factual, this may be an instance where live people witnessed a ghost who, in turn, saw other ghosts.

KITCHEN APPARITION

Georgetown Hotel and Saloon
6260 Main Street
Georgetown 95634
530-333-4013

Looking like an authentic cowboy bar, the musty atmosphere of the Georgetown Saloon takes visitors back to the 19th century. The hand-carved bar, fireplace surround constructed of quartz mined from beneath the building, and a lot of stories told by the bartender and restaurant staff make this place worth the scary, winding drive from Placerville. Added to all of that, it is full of ghosts.

The Georgetown Hotel was constructed in 1849 on ground that lay over one of the largest gold mines in California. It thrived as a bar, restaurant, and brothel that served miners and overnight guests traveling through the country by stagecoach. The hotel also attracted outlaws and cowboys. These ruffians were so accustomed to shooting their pistols when they won a hand of cards that rooms on the west side of the second floor were kept vacant lest someone take a bullet while trying to sleep. Eventually, the owner placed sheets of steel under the beds so the rooms could be rented.

The original structured was partially destroyed in a glorious blaze on July 14, 1852. Fire broke out again in 1856 and 1896. The structure in use today makes use of part of the original building, including the fireplace surround of quartz.

The historic Georgetown Hotel was the scene of wild celebrations of gold discoveries and many gunfights.

The bartender told me that the place is full of ghosts but he offered no specifics. When I inquired about the notorious room 13 he was initially evasive, but after some persuasion he offered some interesting observations. Previous publications made note of the fact that this hotel was one of the few in the western United States that offered a room number 13 for rent. In fact, the intense ghostly activity experienced by guests and staff in this room have put the hotel on the paranormal map of places to visit. Now rooms 13, 14, and 15 have been consolidated to create an apartment for the bartender. When I asked about ghostly activity in the apartment the bartender shrugged and said, "This whole place is so full of ghosts it feels crowded all the time." I did, in fact, feel like the place was crowded even though the bartender and I were the only living souls in the bar at the time I conducted our brief interview.

The ghost most often seen at the Georgetown Saloon and Hotel is believed to be that of a previous owner. Witnesses describe him as having salt-and-pepper hair, tall, dark-complected, about 50 years of age, and always with a pipe in his mouth. This fellow shows up in the kitchen, standing with his hands on his hips as he watches staff prepare meals.

I inquired about the name of this ghost and his history, but no one on the premises could answer my questions. So many people died in the barroom from gunfights, alcoholism, and accidents that the current staff could not isolate a particular individual who might be the authoritative salt-and-pepper ghost. Judging from the ghost's clothing, he lived prosperously in the late-19th century. There is speculation that he died in the fire of 1896 while trying to save his hotel.

The ghostly activity experienced by staff and visitors is intense and constant. It includes slamming doors, migrating cold spots, TVs and lights that go on and off, and knocks on the doors of guestrooms.

OSCAR THE LOVESICK GHOST

American River Inn
Main Street at Orleans Street
Georgetown 95634
www.americanriverinn.com

The remains of 27 miners trapped in the collapsed Woodside Mine had hardly decayed to bone when the historic American River Inn was constructed in 1853 over the site of the tragedy. One of the miners, Oscar, who survived the disaster, took up residence in the new place, known then as the American Hotel, as soon as it opened. Enjoying the sympathy of other miners and the admiration of travelers, Oscar was treated to drinks at the bar and long evenings in the parlor as the center of attention. He entertained eager listeners with stories of giant gold nuggets, dark mines, and the dangers of digging for riches in the high Sierras. With money in his pocket and a degree of celebrity, Oscar also enjoyed the pleasures of a prostitute who lived on the second floor of the boarding house in room 5.

By 1855, things were going well for Oscar. He found work as a carpenter, occasionally found a cache of gold nuggets in nearby creeks, and enjoyed a growing reputation. A chance encounter with a former client of Oscar's girlfriend ended all of that. Responding to Oscar's vehement indignation over his crude comment about the

The ghosts of a man murdered on the steps of the American River Inn and the lover who committed suicide after his death haunt this beautiful Georgetown hotel.

lady's profession, the stranger shot Oscar on the steps of the American Hotel. Heartbroken, Oscar's girlfriend threw herself from the balcony outside her room, landing only a few feet from the place where Oscar died. She died instantly of a broken neck.

The love affair of these two characters must have been intense, because their spirits have yet to leave the boarding house where they lived, loved, and lost their lives.

Several witnesses have seen Oscar's ghost, although, during my last visit on March 24, 2008, the manager claimed she had not experienced anything paranormal during the 11 years she had worked at the inn. Many others have reported details of Oscar's apparition. He appears to be five foot eight inches tall, sports a short beard, and wears tattered clothes. He moves about the inn but shows up most often in room number five and in the second floor hallway. It is said that Oscar likes to whisper in the ears of guests when they are in bed. He has been seen walking through the room from the balcony door to the hall door, switching off the light as he leaves the room. Guest diaries record some fascinating observations.

"In the wee hours of the morning our lamp went on for no reason. We are sure it was Oscar."

"We were in our bed when a dirty-looking miner walked into the room, smiled at us, and left through the door."

Visitors who roam the second floor, or occupy room 5, report hearing a woman's voice.

"In the middle of the night, I awoke to a whisper near my pillow. When I sat up, it was gone. Soon, the whispering was back. I heard a man in the background . . . but it was a woman's voice I heard distinctly."

Some guests have reported seeing a woman dressed in a negligee while she enjoys a drink, smiling at those who notice her. Many believe this is the ghost of Oscar's girlfriend.

Aside from whispers and amazing apparitions, the spirits of the American River Inn like to open and close doors, leave indentations on the quilt-covered beds, and laugh without apparent source.

The inn's Web site boasts the moniker "Pride of the Mountains," and this title is well-earned. In fact, this inn is one of the most beautiful I have ever visited. Beautiful antiques, quilts, window treatments, and wall coverings reproduce the finest décor of the 1850s, creating an ambience that enables even the most skeptical visitor to enjoy lively spirits.

CHRISTOPHER'S GHOST AND OTHER SPIRITED SPIRITS

Sierra Nevada House
835 Lotus Road
Coloma 95613
916-621-1208

For many years the Vineyard House, on Cold Springs Road, was regarded as the most haunted building in Coloma. Featured in many TV shows about ghostly activity, the mansion's history, Gold Rush-era décor, and seclusion offered ghost hunters great opportunities to experience spirits that were not timid in making their presence known. When the Vineyard House was sold and converted from an inn to private residence, ghost hunters had to look elsewhere in Coloma for overnight accommodations that came with spooks. We didn't have to look far. In the heart of historic Coloma, the Sierra Nevada House is

The ghost of a kitchen worker keeps thing moving in the Sierra Nevada House, while a malevolent ghost haunts room four.

the best place to spend the night if you want to carouse with ghosts from the Gold Rush days.

Built in the early 1850s, the Sierra Nevada House was a prime destination for prospectors, businessmen, and mining engineers. Filled with men whose pockets were full of gold nuggets, the hotel also attracted prostitutes, gamblers, and con men. When local gold production declined late in the 19th century, the hotel remained in operation serving land speculators and railroad workers. In 1886, the hotel's owners died and left the establishment to Charles Schulze, who later built the Schulze House on Highway 49. In 1902, Schulze's hotel was nearly destroyed by fire but was quickly rebuilt and re-opened with the addition of a theatre. Fire swept through again in 1925. The present structure stands as it did in 1926 after reconstruction.

Several ghosts haunt the Sierra Nevada House. One is the ghost of a woman who lived in room four and worked in the restaurant. Known for her fiery temper, it is said that she returned to the room one evening to find her boyfriend in the arms of a prostitute. A fight broke out between the women that included yelling and screaming and throwing objects that broke against the walls. As the fight continued, the prostitute got the upper hand and pushed the offended woman onto the balcony and over the railing to her death.

Guests who stay in room 4 often report strange sounds. While sleeping, they hear objects crashing against the walls, the scuffling of feet on the wooden floor, and female voices shouting. Downstairs in the bar, startled customers often see the image of a 19th-century woman appear in the large mirror. In some parts of America, legend has it that mirrors may capture a spirit soon after it leaves the body unless the mirror is covered with black cloth. It appears that the mirror hanging in the Sierra Nevada House bar captured the spirit of the feisty woman who fought for her man in room number four.

Room 4 also has a malevolent ghost named Mark. There are reports that Mark shot his girlfriend in this room in the 1970s. A review of local newspaper archives failed to confirm that this crime took place, but hotel staff told me that the event did happen. This malevolent ghost slams doors and stomps across the room.

A ghost named Christopher keeps himself busy in the kitchen moving things around and hiding knives. He also causes glasses to move across the bar, salt and pepper shakers to slide off the table, and drinks to be spilled. This ghost is known as a prankster, so he might be attracted to stacks of pennies left on a table or a deck of cards.

Other ghosts may be found virtually anywhere in the Sierra Nevada House. Rooms one, three, and four are among the most spiritually active.

CHARLES SCHULZE AND DAISY

The Argonaut
331 State Highway 49
Coloma 95613
530-621-4008

The Schulze House is not a remnant of the Gold Rush era, but it sits amid 36 historic buildings from the 1850s. The house was built in 1916 by Charles Schulze as an enticement for his daughter, Daisy, to

Charles Schulze built this house for his daughter, Daisy, near the gold discovery site in Coloma. Today, it is a popular café and destination for ghost hunters.

move closer to him. Daisy lived near Sacramento, and in 1916 travel into the Sierras was not easy or safe. In order to have more frequent and longer visits with Daisy, Charles Schulze constructed a house which would offer comforts for her and her traveling companions. Schulze was an old-timer in Coloma, having enjoyed success as a miner, blacksmith, teamster, and mason. He was also proprietor of the nearby Sierra Nevada House. Charles died in 1921, leaving all of his property to Daisy.

Daisy used the Schulze House for many years before selling it to local entrepreneurs, who opened a restaurant in her former living room. Over the decades, the building served many businesses. In the 1940s, it was a doctor's office and morgue. Bodies were held in the basement until relatives showed up to take them away. Today, the Schulze House is called the Argonaut, a named given to gold seekers who traveled over-land from the U.S. to California Territory in 1849. The Argonaut offers modern food, but the interior is modeled strictly after 1916 decor. Original wallpaper, floorboards, doorknobs, and bead-board ceiling keep the 21st century from encroaching on the charming place. Added to that, photographs of Daisy and Charles Schulze hang on the walls.

When asked about ghostly activity, the current owner had a lot to say. The odor of split pea soup often pervades the small kitchen and eating area, but that soup is never served at the Argonaut. Perhaps it was Daisy's favorite. Downstairs, shadows play across the walls. One man saw such a distinctive shadow in the stairwell that he thought a co-worker was descending to come help with his work. The shadow descended the stairs, moved across the room, and vanished. Strange shadows are often seen in the eating area at the rear of the building, too.

Local ghost hunter Nancy Bradley reported that a psychic discovered a "wash woman" named Alice in the house. Alice is a large woman who likes the fragrance of espresso. Another sensitive visitor reported the apparition of an elderly man standing at the window overlooking the street. He appeared to be portly, had gray hair, and wore overalls. The photograph of Charles Schulze fits this description.

During my visits to the Argonaut, I always encountered a female presence in the back room. This could be an environmental imprint or residual energy of Daisy or the aforementioned wash woman. I did not see the apparition of this spirit but felt her moving about me, brushing close as if she felt I was standing in her way.

GHOSTS OF THE CHINESE MERCHANT

Wah Hop Store
State Highway 49
Coloma 95613
530-622-3470

Almost everyone I have spoken to about the Wah Hop store in Coloma reports that there is something very strange about the place. From the exterior, it looks like one of many well-preserved, 1850s stone buildings facing State Highway 49 going through the Marshall Gold Discovery State Park. Once you step through the small door, the darkness of the place seems to swallow up visitors, instantly transporting them to another era. The room is filled with paraphernalia sold to

The Wah Hop store in Coloma houses mysterious Chinese spirits from the Gold Rush era that create peculiar fragrances and light anomalies in photographs.

miners, including eating and cooking utensils, Chinese medicine bottles, and other remnants from the Gold Rush era. Many believe the Wah Hop store is also filled with spirits of Chinese miners and other members of hard working but harshly treated minorities.

Each time I enter this building, I feel a drastic change in atmosphere. Regardless of the weather, the air inside the store is cool, musty, and resonates with the muted chatter of people speaking Chinese. Some visitors hear the sound of a meat cleaver hitting the chopping block or glass bottles clinking.

During a recent visit, I found that the light generated by the flash on my digital camera was completely absorbed by the heavy atmosphere inside the store. I moved to another location to check the flash mechanism and found that it worked correctly. Returning to the Wah Hop store, I encountered the same problem; all my photos turned out very dark, as if I hadn't used the flash. I also felt profoundly fatigued during my visits to this building. A few moments outside and my energy returned.

LADY IN BURGUNDY

Pioneer Cemetery
Cold Springs Road
Coloma 95613

Cold Springs Road winds around the wooded hills of Coloma, past several historic sites and buildings left over from the Gold Rush days. As the road descends through the scattered community toward the American River, it separates the haunted Vineyard House (now a private residence) and Coloma's Pioneer Cemetery. The builder of Vineyard House, Robert Chalmers, was the earliest recorded owner of the land on which the cemetery sits. Among those laid to rest in this graveyard are miners, prospectors, explorers, farmers, builders, murderers, and Chalmers himself. It is also the final resting place of Chalmers' wife, Louise, who nursed Robert through the final years of his life, when he went insane from syphilis. Two men executed for murder in front of the Chalmers home on a makeshift gallows also occupy graves in this cemetery. This fascinating collection of dead

The Pioneer Cemetery in Coloma is one of the most haunted places in the Gold Rush country. The famous Lady in Burgundy stands by the road enticing drivers to visit the graves.

residents combines with decaying monuments, steep hillsides, and a dense canopy of sprawling trees to produce a creepy atmosphere even in broad daylight. At night, the place is absolutely terrifying.

Travelers passing by this cemetery at any time of day may see a mysterious woman standing at the roadside, beckoning them to turn into the cemetery. Witnesses report that she is wearing a burgundy dress, a remarkable report since most ghosts appear in black and white or muted colors. Some keen observers add that the woman's rosy cheeks are framed by long black hair, and she appears frantic or upset as she waves to passersby, trying to get them to stop. Some have described the swishing sound of her skirts as she turns away from the road before disappearing. This apparition often makes direct eye contact with piercingly dark eyes, causing many locals to avoid passing by the cemetery when they are alone at night.

Who is this mysterious lady in burgundy? The only clue is that she watches over a plot containing the remains of Charles Schieffer, who died in 1864 at the age of 41; his son, William, who died in 1861 at age 2; and a daughter, May, aged 27 when she died in 1890. Catherine Schieffer, born in 1862 and deceased in 1916, lies in a distant section of the cemetery. It is likely that this ghost is Catherine, sister of William and May and daughter of Charles Schieffer. A report published on the Internet by El Dorado Paranormal Investigations reached a similar conclusion. Several ghost hunters have spotted the lady in burgundy hovering near these graves.

It appears that Catherine Schieffer, the lady in burgundy, has forsaken her own grave and watches over those of her family or else stands at the roadside, looking for help. It is likely that she wants someone to relocate her remains to the family plot.

THE NANNY'S GHOST

Sequoia Restaurant
Bee-Bennett House
643 Bee Street
Placerville 95667
530-622-5222
www.sequoiaplacerville.com

The ghost of a four-year-old boy and the nanny charged with his safekeeping haunt this magnificent Placerville mansion. Both

The ghost of a suicidal nanny haunts the Bee-Bennett House in Placerville. A vortex has been discovered in the women's restroom on the second floor.

of these spirits are quiet and seem happy that their former home is now a popular restaurant and wedding venue, which sometimes accommodates 200 guests caught up in the celebration of a wedding.

Colonel Frederick Bee, who distinguished himself as an attorney and founder of the Placerville-Saint Joseph Overland Telegraph Company and Pony Express service, built the manion in 1853. The colonel also served as Chinese Consul by decree of the Emperor of China. With his celebrity growing beyond the confines of Placerville society, the Colonel sold his home. After a succession of owners, Judge Marcus Percival Bennett (1854-1924) purchased the place in 1889. Bennett and his wife, Mary Cordelia Bennett (1861-1952), upgraded and expanded the home and raised seven daughters and one son in the house.

One day, in 1904, four-year-old Marcus Bennett Jr. was left to the care of a young nanny. While playing on the second floor, Marcus wandered away from his nanny. In a brief moment, he fell down the steep staircase, landing on the fourth step with a broken neck. Attracted to the stair by a loud noise, the nanny was instantly overcome with grief at the death of the little boy and fear of the wrath of the judge.

Four-year-old Marcus Bennett Jr. died in a tragic accident on these steps in the Bee-Bennett House in Placerville.

She retrieved a rope from a downstairs closet, fashioned a noose, and tied the rope to the vertical standards of the second-floor railing. Standing at the top of the staircase, she placed the noose around her neck and pushed off the steps, swinging forward to her death.

During my visit to the Bee-Bennett House, the staff was busy preparing for a wedding and other events, but the staircase and second floor were sufficiently quiet for psychic investigation. After a short time standing at the top of the steep staircase, I could feel Jason's fear as he tumbled down the steps and the anguish of the nanny who discovered his lifeless body. By grasping the crossbeam that spans the staircase and swinging my body over the steps, I felt the environmental imprint of the nanny's great sadness and her fear of passing into the unknown.

Ghost hunters Nancy Bradley and Shannon McCabe—known as the "Ghost Girls"—have investigated this house and found the spirits there to be sufficiently active that they featured it in their TV show.

The ghost of the nanny, or perhaps another female spirit, haunts the second floor rooms used by brides to prepare for their weddings. The spirit moves objects so they can be easily found. She also leaves a rose in a particular place so it is found only by the bride just before she leaves the second floor for her wedding.

The Bee-Bennett House has been modified to serve as a restaurant, but all of the elegant interior woodwork, doorknobs, and fireplace surrounds are original. This offers ghost hunters opportunities to touch objects that may retain the imprints of two prominent families and a young nanny.

Shannon McCabe, president of Northern California's Haunted and Paranormal Investigations (HPI), told me that a vortex exists in the women's restroom on the second floor, near the ballroom. Adventurous souls who dare to stand at the sink close to the door with eyes closed will feel intensely dizzy. I tried this and felt the dizziness together with an intense sensation of being pulled downward.

HALLOWED HAUNTINGS

Placerville Union Cemetery
642 Bee Street
Placerville 95667
www.cagenweb.com/eldorado/cemeteries/union.htm

The Placerville Union Cemetery is one of several fascinating pioneer graveyards in the area. The ground was selected as a graveyard because of its location on a prominent hill, which affords the deceased a view of

Placerville's Union Cemetery contains the remains of many of the town's famous pioneers and forgotten others whose graves are unmarked.

the town, on the north side of a large creek now covered by Highway 50. The first burials took place as early as 1860, but the landowner did not deed the land for use as a cemetery until 1870. By 1871, various associations and social clubs, including the Masons, Odd Fellows, and Druids, had established large sections of the graveyard for exclusive use by their members. In 1947, the cemetery was declared full, but burials continued with the addition of 3,000 more graves over the next 20 years. Creation of these additional graves was made possible by the desecration of older graves, many of them composed of wooden coffins and markers that had deteriorated badly. The disturbance or loss of many graves may be the reason ghost hunters encounter angry spirits here.

Many paranormal experts believe spirits encountered in graveyards are present because of some event that occurred after death. These spirits are not waiting for revenge for some offense they suffered when alive or communication with loved ones, nor do they suffer an inability to leave their bodies. They are present because of the disturbance of their grave. Typically, graves that have been damaged by natural processes, such as floods, fires, landslides, vandalism, looting, or intentional desecration arouse the indignation of the deceased's spirit. Skilled ghost hunters may encounter these ghosts and detect their anger, sadness, disdain, or sense of loss.

In many graveyards, ghost hunters experience paranormal phenomena but that does not indicate the presence of the spirit of a dead person. EVP, EMF spikes, orbs, the sensation of cold spots or a thickened atmosphere, and other bizarre phenomena may be the result of a haunting, which is defined as an environmental imprint or residual energy created by intense, repetitive events performed by the living. If a grieving mother visited the grave of her child frequently for years, always sobbing and pouring out great emotion, an imprint may be created at the site that can be detected decades later. Astute ghost hunters look for the graves of children and young adults who were likely mourned for decades by distraught parents and siblings.

Graves on the steep slope of the Union Cemetery, facing Highway 50, have been productive for those who seek EVP. Try the grave of little Sarah Chichester, who died on May 22, 1877, at eight-years-old. Her monument stands about three feet tall. Your audio recorder may capture the sound of a girl laughing. The grave of 20-year-old Donald "Donnie" Gilman, who was buried in 1995, is next to that of his mother, Patricia Gilman, who died January 30, 2001. EVP have been captured here and sensitive visitors detect intense emotion.

VIRGIL AND THE CLEANING LADY

Cozmic Café
594 Main Street
Placerville 95667
520-295-1481

This popular Placerville café is housed in one of the oldest buildings in town. Constructed in 1859 by John McFarland Pearson out of local stone, the building withstood calamitous events including landslides, floods, and disastrous fires that consumed other nearby structures. A soda works thrived there until the 1930s, generating enough income to support the addition of a second floor in 1897 by Pearson's sons. The abandoned gold mine that extended from the first floor into the hillside provided natural refrigeration, keeping the soda and other commodities, such as syrup, beer, and eggs, cool during the blazing

The Cozmic Café occupies one of the oldest buildings in Placerville and sits at the opening of a former gold mine.

heat of summer. Today, the Cozmic Café serves up natural food, stages live entertainment, and provides a showcase for local wines and beers. It's a lively place that also offers a chance to experience the paranormal.

The mineshaft that extends 135 feet from the rear of the café is haunted by the ghost of a miner. Psychic Rosemary Dean contacted this spirit and learned that his name is Virgil. Virgil was 27 years old when he died in a cave-in. According to Dean, this spirit refuses to acknowledge that he is dead. Virgil remains in the mine because he feels cheated by life and wants to continue his search for riches.

During my visits to the mine I did not encounter Virgil, but several times I felt an unseen being brush past me, leaving a foul odor in the air. Other ghost hunters have captured orbs in digital images and EVP on audio recorders.

People eating at the tables in the mine's large anteroom have been unnerved by unexplained voices coming from deep inside the tunnel. Angry exchanges and shouting have been reported to café staff. When someone enters the mine to investigate, the voices cease.

The second floor of the building is haunted by a ghost who likes to play tricks on visitors. Wearing a straw hat and sporting a handlebar mustache, this spirit moves glassware, pushes menus off the tables, drags chairs across the floor, and spills water. Psychics who have contacted this ghost report that he died of a heart attack while in the building. This fellow likes his disembodied existence and prefers to stay in his former workplace. A female ghost sometimes appears in the same area as the trickster. Witnesses who have seen this ghost report that she is elderly and dressed in late-19th-century clothing. Named Alice by staff and regular customers, this ghost moves about as if she is cleaning the place. She usually appears in the restrooms on the second floor.

TOP HAT GHOST

Chamber of Commerce Building
542 Main Street
Placerville 95667
916-621-5885

The El Dorado Chamber of Commerce building is the hub of modern business in the region, but it is also one of the most haunted places in old Hangtown. Constructed of stone in the 1850s, the building is believed to stand on the site of one of the town's famous hanging trees. Over the years, the building has been renovated many times, but remnants of some of its architectural incarnations are still visible and often linked to ghostly activity.

A mezzanine, accessible via a landing off the staircase, once served as balcony for an orchestra. For many years, people working on the floor below heard creaking floorboards overhead, as if someone were walking around the confined space. Occasionally, people who work in the building have been brave enough to investigate, and some of them have seen the ghost responsible for the noise. He appears as a tall, thin man, dressed in a black suit with a tall hat. There is speculation that this is the same ghost that appears down the street at the Hangman's Tree Bar and Café. Psychic investigation revealed that this ghost is a former executioner named Darrell.

Darrell may appear at the Chamber of Commerce building because the mezzanine approximates the height of the scaffold where he did his grizzly business. I have visited the mezzanine several times over a period of many years. The original railing and floorboards are still in place. It is now crowded with air conditioning and heating ducts and closed off to the floor below by a suspended ceiling. This confined space offers little room for roaming about, but strange sounds still emanate from the area.

One the second floor, remnants of dressing rooms once used by theatre performers still exist in the renovated restrooms. An employee of the Chamber of Commerce showed me these spaces and reported that local ghost hunters have obtained EVP of a woman singing in the shower. On the first floor, the office to the right of the information counter may be haunted, too. Photographs taken in this office often reveal orbs close to the floor. The room sits directly under the mezzanine and may occupy the space where a wagon waited to haul hanged men away for burial. This distasteful job would have been performed by Darrell, the hangman.

GHOSTS OF THE DESPERADOS

Hanging Tree Bar and Café
305 Main Street
Placerville 95667
916-622-3878

The effigy hanging by a noose near a second-story window of this famous bar reminds everyone that Placerville was once called Hangtown. Formerly known as Dry Diggins, the town was renamed Hangtown in 1850 after vigilantes quickly tried four men for robbery, found them guilty, and sentenced them to death by hanging. The sturdy tree selected for use stood on the site where the modern-day Hangman's Tree Bar and Café is. The tree no longer stands, but its stump lies hidden under the floor of the bar. A mural behind the back-bar depicts the tree as it stood in Elsterner's Hay Yard, with a noose ready for use. Another hanging tree was located at 542 Main Street, where the Chamber of Commerce building now stands. Historians believe both trees were used for more than the officially recorded number of hangings—four. It is likely that more than 20 desperadoes and outlaws met their deaths at the end of a rope in Hangtown.

Aside from the hangings that took place at this location, it is believed that several deaths occurred in the bar and in rooms on the second floor. Throughout the 20th century, locals and tourists visiting the Hangman's Tree Bar and Café have reported strange cries, sobbing, and screams that were attributed to the ghosts of men who died by hanging. An eerie green light has been seen here, too, rising from the floor of the bar. One report states that this light emanates from the basement, but a bartender told me there is no basement.

Several apparitions have been spotted inside the bar and on the street in front of the building. According to witnesses, some of the specters resemble miners and gunfighters. The most frequently seen apparition is that of a tall man with a tall hat dressed in dark clothing. This fellow walks through walls, belying his lifelike appearance. A psychic identified this spirit as that of the hangman's assistant, who cared for the tree and prepared the noose.

The bartender can tell you stories of restroom doors that swing open and close by invisible hands, a jukebox that plays tunes without being triggered, and shot glasses that move around the back-bar. If you spend some time sitting at the bar you may find yourself in the company of a person dressed in 19th-century clothing who vanishes before your eyes.

THE WHISTLING GHOST

Cary House
300 Main Street
Placerville 95667
530-622-4271
www.caryhouse.com

Standing at the west end of Main Street, this imposing, four-story, brick building is an elegant reminder of accommodations offered to well-heeled travelers during the 1850s. Opened in 1857 with only three stories, the Cary House offered hot and cold running water in a community bathroom on every floor, a luxurious lobby, and was allegedly fireproof. Its 77 rooms ranged from spacious suites to nice but cramped sleeping quarters for those who scraped enough gold from nearby creeks to treat themselves to a week of fine living in a fancy hotel.

By 1860, the Cary House was known as the finest hotel in Gold Rush country, attracting luminaries such as Mark Twain, Lola Montez, and Horace Greeley. In its first 10 years, more than 90 million dollars in gold bullion passed through its doors as bankers and investment managers used the first floor rooms as a counting house. The place also attracted gamblers, con-men, high-class prostitutes, and others desperate to scratch their way out of the dregs of Placerville society by working for the wealthy or preying on their weaknesses.

All of this made the Cary House a place of high drama. One of the most dramatic events to take place there involved a man named Stan who worked as a desk clerk. Stan made the mistake of falling in love with a lady who was involved with a successful gambler. Failing to conceal his infatuation, Stan aroused the anger of the gambler, who pulled out a gun and shot him at the foot of the stairs. Crawling to the middle of the lobby, Stan died staring at the horrified face of the woman he loved.

Today, the ghost of Stan is said to wander throughout the hotel. He generates cold spots, orbs in photographs, and an eerie presence near the stairs where he was shot.

Nancy Bradley has detected several spirits in the Cary House while conducting tours for paranormal enthusiasts. With more than 50 people in tow, Bradley has found spirit remnants in almost every room on the second and third floors. (The fourth floor was added in the 1970s.) One of these spirits is that of Arnold Wiedman, a teamster who operated a large, horse-drawn wagon for hire. According to Bradley, Wiedman was living in room 212 with his wife and baby daughter when he died of influenza. His ghost is still there, creating cold spots that have been reported by guests who complain of an icy draft.

Room 201 is one of the more paranormally active rooms at the Cary House, with doorknobs that jiggle through the night and the strong scent of lavender often detected outside the door. It is believed that the room is haunted by the ghost of a woman who favored this scent in life. I have heard many reports of ghostly activity that include the scent of lavender. Like water and other simple enticements, lavender may attract spirits.

When I visited the Cary House in February of 2008 with a team of paranormal experts, we encountered unexplained whistling in a long dark corridor on the first floor at the rear of the building. The volume was so loud that I felt that a living person must be whistling nearby, but a thorough search revealed no one who might have generated the sound. The tone of the whistle was of the kind that might be used to attract the attention of a person or a team of horses. An EVP sweep through this area failed to capture disembodied voices.

A HOST OF GHOSTS

Diamond Springs Hotel
545 Pleasant Valley Road
Diamond Springs 95619

The Diamond Springs Hotel serves up great food in its restaurant, but no overnight accommodations are available unless you are a ghost. This 1916 building sits over a vortex that allows spirits from several eras to access the area. According to the manager, Amy, the vortex is near the back booth in front of a large refrigerator. The area looks no different from other parts of the restaurant, but staff and customers have reported numerous paranormal experiences while standing at this spot, including the sensation of being pulled downward, awareness of voices in the nearby vacant restrooms, and a ghostly presence in the corner booth. The wide range of ghostly activity is linked to the history of the land on which the building sits.

For hundreds of years before the first settlers entered the area, Miwok Indians operated a crematorium and large burial ground in the center of modern-day Diamond Springs. Numerous unmarked graves, scattered remains, and desecrated sites sacred to the Miwoks all

The Diamond Spring Hotel no longer accommodates overnight guests, but the restaurant offers good food, energetic ghosts, and a vortex.

contribute to the restless spirits that gather in the hotel and the open lot to its rear. In the late 1840s, John Sutter's men charged with producing roofing materials occupied the site that the hotel sits on today. In 1850, these men were joined by 200 immigrants from Missouri. One of these lucky travelers unearthed one of the largest gold nuggets ever found in the Gold Rush country, weighing in at 25 pounds. Such instant, easy wealth led the immigrants to unanimously decide to develop their campground into a town. Quartz crystals that filled stream beds inspired the name for the new town. As with most Gold Rush towns, buildings sprang up quickly. Also typically for a Gold Rush town, fire ravaged the town in 185. Undeterred, residents rebuilt their homes and stores with stone rather than the highly flammable wood previously used and developed agricultural and lumber businesses.

In the early 20th century, Diamond Springs was in decline when Antone Meyer arrived. Finding cheap land and building materials, he erected a large, two story building. Antone didn't know his new hotel sat on sacred Indian ground, but soon after its opening the place gained a reputation for strange happenings. Local ghost hunters, including Nancy Bradley, and members of American Paranormal Investigations and HPI, have published reports of activity witnessed by staff and customers.

The area around the site of the vortex is highly active. While standing at this site, sensitive people often hear voices emanating from the nearby vacant restrooms. When I performed an EVP sweep of the men's room, I witnessed the toilet stall door swing in a 45-degree arc in both directions. The noise of squeaky hinges was captured on my audio recorder together with the faint sound of laughter. Former employee Nancy Miller reported voices and other nondescript noises in both restrooms as she filled dispensers. Unnerved, she raced through her work and left the rooms as fast as possible while feeling that an unseen being was watching her.

In the booth at the southeast corner of the dining room, a ghostly man and his dog appear. The apparition is that of a tall, bearded man wearing Gold Rush-era clothing. His dog has been described as a black Labrador retriever. Customers who see this man are immediately puzzled as to why he was allowed to enter the restaurant with his dog. When the situation is brought to the attention of staff, they laugh and assure the concerned patron that the man and dog will soon be gone. A psychic determined that the man's name is Matthew and that he died of stomach cancer while on the premises.

Strange odors and sounds may be detected in almost any part of the building. These include the laughter of children, a woman crying, people talking, heavy footsteps, musty odors, the aroma of pipe smoke or odor of a cigar, rattling dishes and glasses, and coins falling onto a table. The ghosts of children like to turn on water faucets and lights and play with kitchen utensils. Upstairs, they run through the narrow hallway, creating the sound of footsteps from four or more children.

Other places to hunt ghosts:
REMAINS OF THE GHOST

Bell's General Store
State Highway 49
Marshall Gold Discovery State Park
Coloma 95613
530-622-3470

The iron doors that stand with the brick remains of Bell's General Store in Coloma may have Gold Rush-era EVP.

Most of the buildings constructed in Coloma in the 1850s were made of wood. A few, including Robert Bell's grain and feed store, were made of brick or stone. In spite of its more durable building materials, the structure is now deemed unsafe and access is forbidden.

Standing at the iron doors, however, ghost hunters have captured EVP on audio recorders, including the sound of a bell ringing when unseen customers enter the establishment. Historical accounts indicate that Robert Bell suspended a small bell over his door that announced the arrival and departure of customers.

RICHES TO RAGS GHOST

James Marshall Monument
Gold Discovery State Park
Coloma 95613

In 1890, the State of California dedicated its first historic monument. It was placed on a hill overlooking the place where James Marshall discovered gold in 1848. The tall monument is capped with a bronze effigy of the man who set off one of the greatest human migrations in history and exposed the unimaginable wealth that brought statehood to California. In spite of this unique role in history, Marshall died penniless on August 10, 1885. His body lies beneath the monument, but his spirit is said to wander about the viewing area. Many visitors have been frightened by the strange shadow that plays across the base of the monument.

APPARITION ON PROSPECTOR ROAD

Between Kelsey Road and Lotus Road
Coloma 95613

Built by Chinese labor in the 1850s, this partially paved road cuts across steep hillsides and connects some tiny enclaves that were once prosperous towns. The ghost of an old prospector, who probably lost his life in the area while searching for gold, appears here. He has been seen by as many as four people simultaneously, who described him as being nearly solid. Most witnesses report that he appears wet and blue from cold, even on warm evenings. This apparition is probably a ghost rather than an environmental imprint, because he makes specific gestures at witnesses such as pointing his finger at them while attempting to speak.

EMPIRE ANTIQUES

432 Main Street
Placerville 95667
530-642-1025

The curved ceiling, great depth and width, and little windows of the projection booth high on the back wall are telltale signs that his building was constructed as a movie theatre. Today, the place is filled with antiques where more than 40 dealers offer the best memorabilia the Gold Rush country has to offer. Ghost hunters have captures orbs in photographs taken at the rear of the store, where a stage and movie screen once stood. If you can visit the store when there is no crowd, you may get in touch with a bygone era by handling some of the fascinating antiques that include weapons, clothing, glassware, and eating utensils.

HIDDEN PASSAGE

352 Main Street
Placerville 95667
530-622-4540

This charming little bookstore has more to offer than fascinating reading materials. The rear wall of the store looks like it was once the front of a building. It features heavy iron shutters covering a large window and door, which typically faced the street for protection against fire. The most bizarre feature of this place is that books sometimes fly off the shelves, as if invisible hands were flinging them to the floor. These books don't just fall; they travel as far as 10 feet horizontally before dropping to the floor.

Chapter 5

The South-Central Gold Diggings:
From Amador City to Jamestown

If James Marshal had not discovered gold at Sutter's Mill in Coloma, any one of several locations along the Stanislaus River, near Sonora, might have become California's historic gold discovery site. Gold discoveries in late 1848 and throughout 1849 drew thousands of 49ers to the area, in 1850 raising the population of Tuolumne County to more than 20,000. In the city of Sonora and small towns like Jamestown, Amador City, and Murphys the Gold Rush-era atmosphere is preserved in quaint streets, hundreds of historic buildings, and rock outcroppings where marks made by miners' picks can still be seen.

Not far from Sonora, Colombia is the best preserved Gold Rush-era town in California. Often used for movies and TV shows, Colombia's inns, shops, and other buildings harbor many ghosts from the 19th century.

GHOSTLY LADY OF THE CANDLES

Hotel Imperial
14202 Highway 49
Amador City 95601
209-267-9172
www.imperialamador.com

After the disastrous fire of 1878 that destroyed most of the Gold Rush-era wooden buildings on Main Street (now Highway 49), Bernardo Sanguinetti constructed a two story brick building with thick walls and a tin roof. This building withstood subsequent fires and the ravages of time and weather, and now houses the beautiful

A ghost waitress works at the stately Imperial Hotel at the head of Amador City's Main Street.

Imperial Hotel. According to Sunset magazine, the hotel has a "seductive opulence" while preserving the rustic charm of the 19th century. Standing at the top of Main Street and offering a fascinating view of the town from its second-floor balcony, the Imperial Hotel is the focal point in Amador City for history buffs and ghost hunters.

Over the years, Sanguinetti's building served as a mercantile store, boarding house, gambling hall, and refuge for homeless miners. With such an array of visitors and residents, it is no wonder the place is haunted. Like ghosts everywhere, the restless spirits in this building play with light switches, open and close doors, and create the creepy feeling that you are being watched. But the Imperial Hotel also has a ghost that appears completely lifelike and interacts with guests in the dining room. This ghost is a woman dressed in 19th-century clothing. She appears at tables in the dining room, talks with guests, takes orders, and then disappears. Guests are then confused when a living waitress shows up to take their order. After mentioning that the order was already given to the lady in the long white dress, they are shocked to learn that there is no other waitress on duty. Hotel staff members are not surprised. Known only as the "lady in white," the ghost waitress does not introduce herself. She resembles the woman whose portrait hangs in the dining room, but there are further clues as to her identity.

The last time I visited the Hotel Imperial, I was told that ghostly activity in the dining room has taken on a new dimension. Staff and guests have witnessed a candelabra float past unoccupied tables. The floating candelabra has been seen in the second floor hallway, too.

I was allowed access to the hotel's basement to investigate strange sounds reported by staff, some of whom are afraid to enter alone. Materials for maintenance and repair of the old building cluttered the flagstone floor, leaving little open space. Soon after entering the basement, I heard the sound of someone walking around the dimly lit space. The muted sound of boots on the stone floor, including the occasional scuff of shoe leather, suggested I was not alone, although I knew I was. I also heard the sound of something being dragged across the floor, as if an unseen worker was moving about an invisible burlap sack of grain. I did not capture light anomalies in my photographs or EVP on my audio recorder, but the sounds I heard were loud and clear and accompanied by the feeling that I was not alone.

GHOST OF THE COMPULSIVE HOUSEKEEPER

The Mine House
14125 Highway 49
Amador City 95601

Millions of dollars in gold passed through the counting rooms of the Mine House Inn in Amador City. The spirit of the building's housekeeper keeps the place neat and clean.

This imposing brick building stands on a ledge overlooking historic Highway 49, facing the abandoned gold mine that brought great wealth to Amador City. Much of the gold mined from the region was brought to this building, which served as the Keystone Mining Company headquarters. Composed of eight rooms, each one was dedicated to some aspect of the mining business. When the place became an inn in 1957, the rooms were given names that memorialized their original purpose. The Vault Room still contains the huge safe where millions of dollars in gold was kept. The Assay Room, Director's Room, and Counting Room have all retained the unique atmosphere created by the activity for which they were used.

In December of 2007, when I last visited the Mine House, I was disappointed to find that it was closed. A caretaker kindly unlocked all the doors and allowed me several hours to investigate the place in which I had previously spent many nights. Standing alone in several of the rooms, I noticed disembodied footsteps, some heavy, as if made by boot-clad feet, while others were light, like the patter of children's bare feet. Over the years, several stories about the ghosts of the Mine House have been published in books and on the Internet. The most active ghost in the building is that of a woman who was once housekeeper for the mining company. Psychic investigation has determined that her name was Sarah. Sarah becomes most active when guests are messy. Her compulsion for neatness causes her to gather discarded clothing or towels into a pile. If she discovered anything left on a bed, she pushes it onto the floor. Guests who have seen Sarah report that she holds a cat in her arms or stands while the cat rubs against her legs.

The ghost of a little girl haunts the Director's Room. It is reported that a girl was accidentally injured on the street in front of the mine and brought to the headquarters for treatment. Unfortunately, she died within minutes of her arrival. Bound to the building or attracted to its cool, dark atmosphere, the girl has haunted it for over 100 years. She has been seen wearing a white pinafore dress and black shoes. During my overnight visits to the inn, I saw her shoes several times as she dashed across my room. I also spotted a portion of the dress on the porch at the rear of the building.

Ghost hunters should watch for the reopening of this building as a country inn. Ghosts tend to become more active after a building has sat vacant for a while, especially if renovations are made.

GHOST OF THE SENATOR

Sutter Creek Inn
75 Main Street
Sutter Creek 95685
209-267-5606
www.suttercreekinn.com

In 1860, after the wild days of the Gold Rush, John Keyes settled in the small, rich town of Sutter Creek. Nestled in the Sierra foothills, Sutter Creek was the perfect blend of excellent climate, accessible transportation to Sacramento, booming economy, and developing society of gentlepeople. Most itinerant prospectors, troublemakers, drunks, and highwaymen were gone by then, and in their place came gentlemen like Keyes. Soon after his arrival in town, Keyes started construction of a fine home for his fiancée, Clara McIntyre, who would soon arrive from New Hampshire. Anticipating Clara's reluctance to leave her New England home and lifestyle, Keyes built a house for her that resembled a New England-style cottage. Their life together was short and marred by the death of their only child from diphtheria. Not long after that, John died, making Clara a widow at 34.

Being alone and well established in Sutter Creek, Clara was much sought after by suitors, one being State Senator Edward C. Voorhees. Edward married Clara on March 29, 1880, in the rose garden behind the house John Keyes built. The couple had a son who died in WWII and a daughter, Gertrude, who lived in the house until the age of 90. In her final years, she sold the place for use as a nursing home.

In 1996, Jane Way purchased the property, added additional rooms, and opened the place as the Sutter Creek Inn. Not long after welcoming her first guests, Jane was visited by the ghost of Edward Voorhees. Appearing lifelike and decked out in a cut-away coat and tall hat, the senator spoke to Jane. Obviously pleased with the renovations and new owner, the ghost said, "I will protect your inn."

Jane thought the man who spoke to her was a guest dressed for a costume party, but when he vanished before her eyes she knew the inn was haunted. Later, when leafing through a stack of old photographs, she spotted a picture of Senator Voorhees and recognized him as the man who spoke to her. Some time later, the apparition of Gertrude Voorhees appeared. Moving about the parlor, Gertrude's ghost inspected the furniture and decorations like she was concerned about the changes that had been made to her home. Staff members of the inn believe Gertrude is pleased, because she does not move or break things the way unhappy ghosts often do.

Guests of the inn don't seem to be bothered by these ghosts. Indeed, many visitors come to the inn seeking an experience with the ghosts of the senator, his daughter, or any of the other ghosts who roam the quaint town. During my visits to the inn, I found orbs in my photographs and EVP of disembodied footsteps in the kitchen. A staff member told me that most of the ghost hunters who visit find the main floor guestroom to be the most active. During Gertrude's later years, she used this room as her bedroom. Ghostly activity in this room may be an indication that Gertrude is still watching over her mother's home.

GHOSTS IN THE MIRRORS

National Hotel
2 Water Street Jackson 95642
209-223-0550

At the head of the oldest street in Jackson, the National Hotel sits near springs that were used by Native Americans as a gathering place for social and religious events. In 1849, the gold seekers used the springs as a rest area and meeting place. Noting the popularity of the place and the year-round abundance of water, an enterprising businessman constructed a wooden building and opened a boarding house and bordello. In 1862, that building burned down. It was quickly replaced by a three-story brick and mortar structure that has withstood the passage of nearly 150 years. The building still stands today, offering overnight guest accommodations decorated with Gold Rush-era décor and antiques, plus several ghosts.

Members of Haunted and Paranormal Investigations of Northern California estimate that as many as 30 spirits haunt the National Hotel. Their investigations confirmed reports by hotel staff members and guests over many years that ghosts here are active.

Among the most active spirits are the ghosts of a little boy, age eight

Several mirrors in the second-floor sitting area of the National Hotel, in Jackson, may have captured the spirits of former residents.

years, and his three-year-old sister. The pair has been spotted playing in the hallways and foyer of the second floor, and in the some of the rooms. A psychic encountered the children in rooms 55 and 44. Spirits of an adult man and woman were also detected in room 55. The children sometimes have a canine companion, a terrier–cocker mix.

In room 47, also known as the Bordello Room, ghost hunters have felt invisible hands pull their hair and touch their arms. Several cold spots have been found, orbs have turned up in photographs, and disembodied whispers have been heard. EVP recordings indicate that the spirits in this room were speaking directly to ghost hunters, calling them by name.

The ghost of a woman has been seen walking the hallways and the second-floor foyer. She is dressed in a 1920s-era orange dress. Witnesses describe her as appearing intoxicated and very friendly. Another female spirit, dressed in blue and white, roams the same area. She is described as tall, elegant, and refined.

Male spirits in the hotel have been known to speak to astonished guests and ghost hunters. One spirit appears dressed in cowboy clothing. Another spirit, notorious for his offensive language, wears a black coat, white shirt, and string tie. Other male spirits include men dressed as miners, a teenage boy, and two men dressed in 1920s-era suits.

A good location for surveillance of ghostly activity is the second floor foyer. In this space, five antique mirrors face the center of the foyer. Every time I have visited the National Hotel I have seen faces of spirits in all five mirrors. Attempts to capture these images with a film or digital camera have not been successful. Ghost hunters who sit quietly for a few minutes will see amazing images in these mirrors suggesting spirits have been captured by them.

GHOST OF THE LADY'S MAN

Hotel Leger
8304 Main Street
Mokelumne Hill 95245
209-286-1401
www.hotelleger.com

At the age of 35, George Leger (pronounced luh-zhay) left his home

The ghosts of hotel builder George Leger and several other Gold Rush-era characters haunt this popular Mokelumne Hill inn.

in Alsace-Lorraine for California's fabled Gold Rush country. Arriving in Mokelumne Hill in 1851, Leger purchased land on Main Street, and began construction of a hotel that was little more than wooden walls topped by a large tent, supported, in part, by the adjacent courthouse. In 1854, a fire destroyed it, leaving only the foundation and stone walls of the courthouse. With steadfast devotion to his dream of a grand hotel, Leger cleared away the rubble and built the Hotel Leger, incorporating the foundation and walls of the old courthouse into the new structure. In 1855, Leger's elegant hostelry, dubbed the "Queen of the Mother Lode," opened its doors and quickly became an oasis for genteel society in a town infamous for gunfights, murders, unsavory bars and brothels, and bandits like Joaquin Murrieta. At one time, 17 murders took place in a period of 17 weeks.

The Hotel Leger was destroyed by fire once again in 1875. Leger was devastated, but a year later he reopened with a grand celebration that featured champagne imported from France and oysters from San Francisco Bay.

George lived in his beautiful hotel with his wife, Louise, so he could look after every detail. The town census in 1860 indicates that the couple had two children. Louise died that year (1833-1860), possibly while giving birth to a third child. In 1870, city records do not list Louise Wilkin Leger, but records indicate Leger had three children, the youngest named Louisa. It is likely Leger's wife died in the hotel. Her grave can be found in Mokelumne Hill's Catholic cemetery.

As a widower, Leger was known as a womanizer. Legend says he was murdered outside his room in 1881 by the jealous husband of a woman whose charms he could not ignore. Local historians insist he died of natural causes in 1879. Regardless of the cause of his death, it seems that nothing can separate him from his beloved hotel and its guests. Leger's ghost has made it clear that he continues to take a strong interest in the place.

New employees are tested with pranks and nerve wracking ghostly phenomena. Locked doors are found open, and open doors are slammed shut and locked by unseen hands. Tools and equipment move; lights turn on and off. One workman witnessed a window fly open, drawers in a dresser open and close, and a Bible float across a room. Visitors have heard snoring from an empty bed, creaking floors boards in empty hallways, and seen the full apparition of George Leger.

One of the hotel's former owners told me she frequently experienced George's presence. Working alone in her office late at night, she felt more secure with the ghost around and thought of him as a guardian. She even enjoyed his bizarre antics that included the sudden appearance and disappearance of a yellow balloon tied to a banister.

Ghostly activity in George's room, number seven, has been reported by several hotel staff and visitors. The empty rocking chair moves as if George is still there watching the hotel's guests, and the door slams shut if left open too long. Rumpled bed sheets appear as if someone slept in the empty bed. I spent a sleepless night in George's room waiting for his spirit to show up. I saw no apparition, but the entire room was freezing cold.

In December of 2007, I spent a night in the hotel with my son Michael. Being the only living souls there, we anticipated a lot of ghostly activity. Outside of our room being freezing cold all night, we had few experiences with the paranormal. EVP sweeps of every room yielded no supernatural audio phenomena. We did hear footsteps on the wood floor, though, intermittently throughout the night. These were loudest outside our room, number 7, formerly George Leger's bedroom.

Aside from the dashing former owner, there may be other ghosts haunting the Hotel Leger. A mysterious woman has been seen descending the stairs past the framed picture of George Leger. In room 2, a woman dressed in elegant Victorian clothing appears. In room 3, the ghost of a little boy crawls around on the floor. In many of the rooms, beds are found unmade and the blankets scattered. Beneath the main floor of the hotel is the basement, called the "dungeon" by staff because it is composed of rooms that once served as jail cells for criminals awaiting trial in the old courthouse. Apparitions of drunken men have been seen here, languishing in chains bound to the stone walls.

BLACK BART AND OTHER GHOSTS

Murphys Hotel
457 Main Street
Murphys 95247
209-728-3444
www.murphyshotel.com

The Murphys Hotel was built in 1856 by James Sperry and John Perry as a hotel, restaurant, and bar for successful miners and travelers using the Matteson Stage Service. This massive stone, brick, and concrete building stands to this day exactly as it did when the Gold Rush was at its peak. With walls as thick as three feet and heavy iron shutters over the windows and doors, the building withstood fires, storms, and rowdy miners who fired shots from their pistols as they celebrated their gold strikes in the creeks around Murphys, a town named for two brothers. With a spacious bar, good food, and genteel accommodations on the second floor, the Murphys Hotel attracted such celebrities as Mark Twain, John Jacob Astor, Horatio Alger Jr., and former president Ulysses S. Grant. The hotel also attracted outlaws such as Black Bart and Joaquin Murrieta. Visitors may stand at the bar in the very place these personalities quenched their thirst. Sensitive people who stand at the end of the bar nearest the street notice peculiar cold spots.

Having spent a total of more than 20 nights in the Murphys Hotel, I can tell you that the second floor is one of the most spiritually active places in the Gold Rush country. I have seen the boot-clad legs of a man, visible from mid-thigh down, walk down the hallway. Others who have seen this apparition believe the legs belong to Black Bart. I have seen this apparition more than 10 times, and many of these sighting took place when the hallway was well lit.

Several other misty, partial apparitions have been spotted in every room on the second floor. Some of these are clearly female, as skirts are seen or heard swishing as the lady walks. Many overnight guests have awakened to the sensation that someone had entered their room. One evening, while seated on the balcony overlooking the street, I watched as the apparition of a well-dressed man appeared. This well-heeled gentleman wore a long, dark, dress coat and tall hat. I watched him for two minutes as he looked over the street scene below, then vanished.

Several other Gold Rush-era buildings in the town of Murphys are good places to seek spirits. The general store across the street from the Murphys Hotel has an eerie atmosphere. It isn't hard to imagine the ghosts of long-dead pioneers relaxing on the steps or porch of the old store. You can visit nearby Mercer Caverns for an underground experience where the spirits of lost cave explorers and Indians wander in the darkness.

REBECCA'S GHOST

Dorrington Hotel
3431 Highway Four
Dorrington 95223
209-795-5800
www.dorringtonhotel.com

For many years I traveled Highway 4 to Bear Valley for skiing, always stopping at the Dorrington Hotel for a short break so my companions and I could use the restrooms and get some coffee. After five or six years of stopping at the hotel several times during ski season, I discovered that it was haunted quite by accident. After a heavy snowfall, I stopped for my usual break only to discover that the long driveway was still packed with snow. Rather than press on, I parked at the side of the highway, slipped on my boots, and hiked through deep snow to the hotel's porch. After that difficult hike, I was disappointed to find the door locked, and no one responded to my knocks. I began looking around for someone, and when I came to the back stair, I started to climb, thinking that a staff member might be upstairs. Halfway up the stairs I looked up and saw a middle-aged woman standing about eight stairs above me. She was dressed in a long brown skirt and blouse with billowing sleeves. I thought it was odd that she wasn't wearing a coat since it was quite cold. As I looked at her she said, "No one's home." Then she vanished.

A few years later, while talking to a waitress at the hotel, I learned about the ghost of Rebecca Dorrington Gardner. Rebecca's husband, John Gardner, arrived at the Sierra Nevada from Scotland in 1850 and purchased 160 acres of land. A cold water spring on the property enabled him to establish a thriving sheep ranch and a popular rest stop for miners. In 1851, Rebecca traveled alone from Scotland and joined John at the ranch, where the two built the hotel that stands on the property today.

John died in Angels Camp on October 12, 1897, at the age of 76. Rebecca lived until 1910, dying at the age of 83 in Altaville. Although these two pioneers died elsewhere, many believe their ghosts haunt the hotel they poured their efforts into.

Stories about Rebecca's ghost can be found at the hotel's web site and other Internet sources. Aside from my sighting, staff and visitors have heard disembodied footsteps, the sound of a woman sobbing in the hallway, and eerie voices that emanate from the walls. Strange shadows have been spotted in many of the guest rooms, lights flash off and on, curtains move, doors slam, and locks are tripped. Rebecca moves objects if she does not like their placement, and has been known to push decorative items off tables, including small Christmas trees.

A less active, male ghost is believed to be John Gardner. His presence is often accompanied by the odor of Bengay. The disembodied sound of children talking and laughing has been heard upstairs. The Gardners' raised four children in this house and, although they died elsewhere, their spirits may have retuned to their beloved home in the mountains, especially since their mother's spirit is also in the house.

There are several reports of Rebecca's ghost making appearances outside the building. There is a rumor that Rebecca died on the back steps, in the location where I saw her ghost. In fact, several astonished guests have reported to hotel staff that they saw a woman fall down the stairs. Rebecca may have suffered an accident on the steps, but she died of natural causes in Altaville.

BED WITH A GHOST

City Hotel
Columbia State Historic Park
22768 Main Street
Columbia 95310
209-532-1479
www.columbiagazette.com/cityhotel.htm

Until 1970, when a mysterious antique bed was placed in a second-floor guestroom, the 1856 City Hotel was not known to be haunted. Soon after the massive carved headboard, bed frame, and footboard was assembled and fitted with bedding, staff and guests began reporting strange experiences.

In the 1870s, the ornate bed was brought overland from the Midwest by a wealthy man who intended to give it to his fiancé as a wedding gift. After establishing a residence and business in Columbia, the gentleman sent for his bride, and she embarked on the difficult journey to California from her home in Ohio. Legend has it that the lady died en route, leaving the gentleman so despondent that he vowed never to marry. Having no use for a wedding bed, it was sent to a warehouse in San Francisco and forgotten until many years after the owner's death. Eventually, the

Columbia's historic City Hotel and its restaurant are haunted by several female ghosts.

bed passed through the hands of antique dealers, then mysteriously returned to its original destination, Columbia. Many believe that a ghost came with the bed.

According to Hoyt Elkins, operations coordinator for the City Hotel since 1970, guests who have slept in the bed, in room number one, have reported mournful sighs, rose-scented perfume, unexplained cold spots, opening and closing of the door, and rattling of the door's security chain. A group of midwives who visited the room sensed intense sadness and offered the suggestion that a woman died in the room during childbirth.

Ghost hunters suspect that two female ghosts account for the paranormal activity in room one and in the parlor. One of these has been named Elizabeth by hotel staff. During séances and Ouija board sessions, psychics independently came to the conclusion that a female spirit present at these sites was named Elizabeth. These and other investigations suggest that Elizabeth died in room 1 during childbirth. Sensitive guests feel her pain and sadness. When I stayed in room 1 and slept in the ornate wedding bed, I was kept awake most of the night by muted sobbing, loud sighs, and occasional gasping as though

The ornate bed that stands in room 1 is believed to be haunted by a ghost named Elizabeth, who died during childbirth.

someone was suffocating. Elizabeth, has been spotted in the parlor outside room 1.

The other spirit in that room is believed to be the woman who was to receive the bed as a wedding gift. Although she died hundreds of miles from Columbia, her spirit seems to have found the bed and become attached to it.

Room 6 is also spiritually active. Guests detect a weird, unseen presence and sometimes witness a doorknob turned by invisible hands. This ghost may be a spirit remnant from the days when the second floor of the City Hotel was a music hall.

The restaurant of the City Hotel may be haunted, too. Many years ago, my wife and I had dinner there with our two-year-old son, Sam. As soon as we sat down, Sam started crying. Ruling out all possibilities of his discomfort, we had to take turns eating while one of us occupied Sam on the porch. A waitress assured us that problems such as ours happened often. She attributed the incessant crying of young children to their ultra-sensitivity to all the spirits in the hotel restaurant.

GHOST OF THE BURNED PRISONER

Old Tuolumne County Jail
158 West Bradford Avenue
Sonora 95370
209-532-1317
www.tchistory.org

The Tuolumne County History Museum could not ask for a better place to display artifacts and recount stories of the region's wild days in the 19th century. Housed in the old jail, the museum has a musty atmosphere and peculiar shadows from muted light penetrating the old windows. Dark jail cells, iron bars and shutters on the narrow windows, and thick, brick walls keep the 21st century out, giving ghost hunters a chance to feel the texture of the 1850s.

The building was constructed in 1857 of locally produced bricks and locally quarried granite. Eight cells, placed at the rear of the building, were only accessed through the sheriff's living quarters and office that fronted the street. The jail was rebuilt in 1865, after a disastrous fire that killed a prisoner and created a ghost.

On December 20, 1865, prisoner Tom Horn felt the chill of the evening and a deep frustration at finding himself in jail for the fifth time in two years. Earlier that afternoon, a friend had tossed a small package through Tom's cell window with matches, a bag of tobacco, and a few papers for rolling cigarettes. After a cold supper, Tom started a fire in his cell. Some say that the fire was an accident. The straw and burlap mattress in the cell would have burst into flame if a few sparks from a carelessly handled cigarette had landed on it. The local newspaper claimed Tom started the fire as a protest against the poor food and cold cell. The truth will never be known, because the mattress exploded in flames, killing Tom Horn in the ensuing blaze.

Today, an effigy of Tom stands in the cell, together with a replica of the mattress. Sensitive visitors who enter the cell can feel the change in atmosphere. Some smell smoke and dash out of the cell choking. Others cannot stay in the cell for more than a few seconds because of a strong odor. The horror of Tom's predicament, whether accidental or in protest, has left residual energy in the cell.

THE UNKNOWN GHOST

Gunn House
286 South Washington Street
Sonora 95370
209-532-3421
www.gunnhousehotel.com

According to an Internet article by Cheri Sicard, the ghost that haunts this historic building is not timid about expressing his disdain for certain guests. Male guests have been thrown from their beds in the middle of the night by strong, unseen hands. The startled guests could not identify a reason for this eccentric bit of ghostly hostility, but there is speculation that this spirit was jealous. He may have been attracted to the men's female bedmates and decided to scare the "competition" away.

The identity of the string ghost is not known but many suspect it is the ghost of the inn's namesake and builder, Dr. Lewis C. Gunn. Gunn came to the Sonora area seeking gold but failed to find a glory hole or rich claim. Instead, he discovered the natural riches and beauty of the region. He also discovered the severe shortage of physicians in Sonora. With his meager bag of gold dust, Gunn built a two-story adobe house and resumed his practice of medicine. He also established the region's first newspaper and began publishing weekly editions. This enterprise did not last long, though. After one of his notoriously scathing editorials an angry crowd burst into Gunn's home and destroyed his printing equipment. Several years later, after Gunn's death, the building was used as the county's hospital. Records are not available, but it is certain that many people died in rooms now used to accommodate overnight guests. Late in the 19th century, Josephine Bisordi purchased the building, expanded it, and opened the Italian Hotel. In the 1960s, the building underwent major renovation, awakening the spirits of the old hospital, including the ghost of Dr. Gunn.

In 2004, owner Shirley Sarno reported that strange things happened around the inn almost everyday. Items fell from kitchen shelves or turned up missing only to be found days later in strange places. Doors open and close by unseen hands. Staff members sometimes have trouble getting unlocked doors open, as if an invisible being is holding the door shut.

The Gunn House has been visited by local ghost hunters and psychics. Room three was found to yield the highest EMF ratings. Guests who stay in room 12 often report the apparition of a tall man standing at the foot of the bed.

FLO THE FRIENDLY GHOST

National Hotel
18183 Main Street
Jamestown 95327
209-984-3446
www.national-hotel.com

Most of the hotels in Gold Rush country have a ghost or two, but few have a ghost as nice as Flo. Staff of the National Hotel named the ghost, and she seems to like the moniker. Some claim she answers to the name by responding to requests to produce EVP or demonstrate her presence by other ghostly activity. Notebooks in each of the rooms are full of reports made by guests about their experiences with the paranormal in this charming hotel. It isn't clear how long Flo has been

Flo the friendly ghost haunts the homey National Hotel in Jamestown.

active in the hotel, but the owner, Stephen Willey, has been receiving reports about her for nearly 30 years.

Built in 1859, the National Hotel is one of the 10 oldest continually operating hotels in America. Meticulous renovations and restorations have preserved the Gold Rush-era charm while updating accommodations to modern standards.

Flo seems to like the second-floor hallway and rooms, but she has also been spotted on the first floor, in the dining room. This ghost is a prankster, dumping guest's clothing on the floor, playing with light switches, turning water faucets on and off, and moving chairs and tables around in the dining room. In the wintertime, when the hotel's heaters were running, housekeepers have entered rooms and found them icy cold. This ghost also likes to slam doors, hide objects, and fill a room with the sound of her laughter.

No one knows much about Flo's identity or why she haunts the National Hotel. The hotel's web site includes a short historical note by a local writer that suggests Flo came west to meet her fiancé, John Davies, who worked for the railroad. Arriving in town in the late 1890s, Flo found that her fiancé, who was deep in gambling debts, had disappeared. While staying at the National Hotel, Flo questioned everyone in town, particularly railroad workers, but could uncover no information that might reveal Davies' whereabouts. Four weeks after her arrival in Jamestown, Flo could not accept the possibility that her fiancé had died or fled. Broken hearted, she left a note on the nightstand that said "Dearest John, I love you so much and will never give up searching for you." In the morning, her lifeless body was discovered with no apparent cause of death. This tragedy may account for the disembodied sobbing that has been heard in the second-floor hallway.

A GATHERING OF SPIRITS

Willow Steakhouse
18723 Main Street
Jamestown 95327
209-984-4338

This remnant of a once-great hotel may be the most haunted building in Gold Rush country. Built over a gold mine (that caved in early in the 1850s) and the foundation of a hotel (built in 1855 and destroyed by fire in 1863), the Willow Steakhouse is a one-story structure crowded with the ghosts of people who died on this location.

The building that exists today was the original ground floor of a two-story hotel constructed in 1869 by John Pereira. With 20 rooms, a popular bar, and the best restaurant in town, the Willow Hotel served miners, gamblers, and railroad workers, some of whom were murdered or committed suicide in the bar and guestrooms. The families of owners also lived and died on the premises. In the latter half of the 19th century, at least three fires destroyed large portions of the Willow Hotel. It was always rebuilt quickly, often with additions that expanded the hotel's facilities. The last fire occurred on July 21, 1975. So much damage was done to the second floor that the building was renovated into a single-story structure that houses the current bar and restaurant. Even without rooms to let, the place was known as the Willow Hotel for several years, until 1994 when the name was changed officially to the Willow Steakhouse and Saloon.

The Willow Steakhouse, plagued by fires, murders, fatal accidents, and suicides, sits over an abandoned mine that caved-in during the 1850s, entombing 20 miners.

Based on credible reports by respected psychics and ghost hunters, it is estimated that there are more than 30 ghosts in this building. Before the first structure was built on this site, a mine cave-in killed thirty miners. As many as 20 ghost miners may roam the bar.

Many other calamities also occurred to trap ghosts at this location. In one second-floor room, two men committed suicide on consecutive nights. A third man was hanged in his room by a mob of vigilantes. For decades, this room was known to be an uncomfortable place where guests often felt frightened. Local lore claims that the great fire of 1975 started in this room. In 1928, owner Gus Ratto retired to his second-floor room one night and shot his wife before turning the gun on himself. The ghosts of these people have been spotted walking in the restaurant. One of them has been described as bald, wearing pajamas, with an angry expression on his face. In the 1890s, an enraged husband murdered his wife in the bar, where her ghost is seen, complete with red hair.

Customers seated at the bar sometimes notice a good-looking man standing close to them. He is dressed in a three-piece suit and white shirt with a black string tie. Sporting an impressive mustache and wearing a fancy black hat, he appears lifelike, but disappears moments after nudging customers. It is believed that this is the ghost of a gambler who was shot in the bar.

At virtually every location in the Willow Steakhouse, ghost hunters have encountered paranormal activity ranging from apparitions to strange sounds that include laughter, sobbing, moaning, whispering, footsteps, glasses clinking, children chanting, a baby crying, and glass breaking. The ghosts there also play with light switches, move objects off the restaurant tables, and turn water on in the restrooms.

Much of the ghostly activity in this building has been attributed to spirits who lost their lives when the structure burned. Some of those spirits were not in the building at the time of their death, however. It has been said that during one of the fires that swept through Jamestown in the 19th century, structures surrounding the Willow hotel were blown up with dynamite to stop the flames from destroying the town's finest building. This was done so hastily and with such inadequate warning that some people were killed inside their homes and shops. Their angry ghosts may have caused subsequent fires that ended the lives of patrons, workers, and owners of the Willow Hotel.

ST. GEORGE HOTEL

16104 Main Street
Volcano 95689
209-296-4458
www.stgeorgehotel.com

The St. George Hotel, in the tiny town of Volcano is off the beaten track for most ghost hunters, but it's worth the time it takes to leave the main highways and travel a winding road to spend an evening, or a night, communing with its spirits. Ghostly activity at this old hotel is so well-documented that a major gathering of ghost hunters took place there in March of 2008. More than a hundred ghost hunters, including members of TAPS and other prominent members of the paranormal field, attended a weekend program of meetings, séances, and spirit hunts.

Named for the saint who killed the demon fire dragon, the St. George Hotel was constructed in 1862 by B. F. George. Its two predecessors, the Eureka Hotel and Empire Hotel both burned to the ground in 1853 and 1859, respectively. Built of brick and mortar, with 14-inch-thick walls, the St. George Hotel has withstood the ravages of time and undergone several renovations that have kept its ghosts curious and active.

The ghosts of the St. George Hotel have been seen by guests and staff members. Two of them, appear so lifelike that guests have reported that they had conversations with Gold Rush-era re-enactors dressed in period costume. When hotel staff informed them that no such re-enactors were on the property, a shaky feeling swept over them as they realized they had spoken to a ghost.

A gentleman in a tall hat with a cane in his hand has chatted with guests, informing them that his name is Charles Osgood. Referring to hotel records, co-owner Richard Winters verified that Charles Osgood was a frequent guest in the late-19th century. Osgood may be responsible for disembodied footsteps in the hallways, creaking floorboards, eerie voices in whispered conversations, and beds that are disturbed after maids finish their work.

The ghost of a little girl roams the hotel, too. A guest staying in a room called "Soldier's Gulch" encountered the little girl, who was wearing a white dress. A brief conversation ended when the little girl vanished before the eyes of the astonished guest.

Diaries kept in every room reveal several paranormal encounters ranging from lifelike apparitions to unexplained cold spots, movement of objects, lights, shadows, failure of electrical devices, and knocking sounds emanating from the walls in response to questions.

Other places to look for ghosts:

GHOST KID

Fallon Hotel
11175 Washington Street
Columbia 95310
209-532-1470

The ghost of a little boy has been seen in room 3 and the second-floor hallway of this 1857 hotel. This playful little guy likes to take toys from other kids and hide them. A psychic investigating the Fallon Hotel has seen this ghost. When I stayed in room 3 with my two-year-old son, he ran around the room all evening as though he was playing with another kid. After hours of this play, my son would not go to sleep. He kept staring at various places within the room as if he saw someone moving around. In rooms 1 and 6, furniture moves about. Guests have reported apparitions walking through their rooms, strange noises, and cold spots. The apparition of a female ghost, believed to be a maid, appears in several rooms, notably rooms 9 and 13.

GHOST OF THE THEATRE OWNER

Fallon Theater
11175 Washington Street
Columbia 95310
209-532-4644

The ghost of theatre builder James Fallon has been seen roaming about his 1886 music hall. Dressed in a long coat and tall hat, Fallon's ghost also generates the odor of cigar smoke that has been detected throughout this building where smoking is prohibited. Staff and visitors who make solo visits to the theatre often hear disembodied voices in animated discussions similar to the din of conversation that fills playhouses and concert halls before performances.

THE OLD BARN

Stevenot Winery
26900 San Domingo Road
Murphys 95247
209-728-3436
www.stevenotwinery.com

On the grounds of this award-winning foothills winery, two miles outside of Murphys, stands an old barn where a local Indian was hanged by a crowd of angry miners. Stop at the winery's tasting room for permission to visit this haunted place. Sensitive people hear a rope turning on a wood beam as if an unseen body was swinging at the end of a hangman's noose.

AMADOR CITY CEMETERY

Behind Imperial Hotel
Church Street at Cross Street
Amador City 95601

The beautiful courtyard at the rear of the Imperial Hotel features a steep stair cut into the hillside that leads to a spooky cemetery. Weeds, tall grass, broken headstones, and grave surrounds that have fallen into disrepair make the place look neglected, but a few graves are decorated with fresh flowers. Ghost hunters who stay at the Imperial Hotel find this graveyard a great place to hang out in the evening, doing EVP sweeps, snapping pictures, or trying to attract the attention of a spirit.

TUOLUMNE COUNTY COURTHOUSE

41 West Yaney Street
Sonora 95370
209-533-5563

Built in 1898 on the site of a former courthouse, notorious criminals have been brought to justice in the halls of this edifice. Built of locally quarried stone and adorned with brass fixtures, this fascinating building has a musty atmosphere, particularly where the staircase meets the ground floor. Look for the partial apparition of an entity covered by a black robe. This may be the ghost of a judge. Also, listen for the clanging sound of chains being dragged along the floor. This may be a remnant from prisoners who were brought here for trial.

The Tuolumne County Courthouse is haunted by the ghosts of a judge and the prisoners convicted in his courtroom.

PROTESTANT CEMETERY

West Center Street and Miwok Trail
Mokelumne Hill 95257

Look for the grave of Louise Leger (1833-1860). Her monument is inscribed in German and flanked by two tall trees. She seems angry that her grave was not visited often by her husband, hotel owner George Leger. A photograph of Louise's headstone may be seen at www.hotelleger.com.

STERLING GARDENS BED AND BREAKFAST INN

18047 Lime Kiln Road
Sonora 95370
888-533-9301
www.sterlinggardens.com

The charming B&B was constructed on the site of the former Kincaid Gold Mine. Naturally, any ghost that turns up here would be suspected to be a miner, engineer, or businessman associated with the mining industry. The brutal reality of the Gold Rush country mines often took the lives of the men who worked them. Fires, cave-ins, gas leaks, transportation malfunctions with mine carts or elevators, and accidents with dynamite or a rusty pick were responsible for hundreds of deaths if not thousands of deaths. The ghost seen at the Sterling B&B stands at the edge of the road near the mailbox, as though waiting for a stagecoach or carriage. Witnesses report that he is friendly but does not speak.

CHAPTER 6

The Southern Gold Diggings:
Chinese Camp to Mariposa and Hornitos

Chinese Camp was originally founded in 1849 by veterans of the Washington Brigade, which saw action in the Mexican-American War, and who called the settlement Washington Camp. Soon after its inception the first Chinese laborers arrived, having been expelled from nearby Camp Salvado due to racial tension between themselves and the Salvadorian miners who worked the diggings. By 1854, the Chinese population exceeded 4,000 and the town was officially renamed Chinese Camp in homage to the large number of Chinese miners who worked claims given up as worthless by Anglo and Hispanic miners only to become rich off their perseverance. The industrious Chinese brought their families to the town and established Joss houses (temples for the worship of their native deities and folk heroes) and stores that offered Chinese foods and herbal medicines.

Named in 1806 when Mexican soldiers witnessed vast swarms of butterflies there, Mariposa later became famous as one of the richest towns of the Gold Rush country. Mariposa's location at the southern end of the Mother Lode accounts for its important economic links with Los Angeles that fostered that city's growth. Today, Mariposa is mainly passed through as the gateway city to the world-famous Yosemite Valley, but its Gold Rush-era history is preserved in buildings and special events.

Hornitos is remote from main highways, but it is well worth a visit. In 1848, it was so small, composed of only a few Mexican miners and ranchers, that it was never even named. With the discovery of gold in the Sierras, the population swelled to 6,000, was named for the dome-shaped tombs of early Hispanic settlers that resembled Mexican ovens, and developed a reputation for fiestas, gambling, and violence. Gunfights were a daily occurrence on the streets of this wild-west town, filling the graveyards with outlaws and innocent bystanders. Today, much of Hornitos is composed of decaying structures that give it the appearance of a genuine ghost town.

GHOSTS OF THE TONG WARS AND OTHER SPIRITS

The Old Post Office
Main Street at Solinsky Alley
and Red Hills Road at J-59
Chinese Camp 95309

With a current population of only 146, the ghosts of Chinese Camp probably outnumber living souls. Founded in 1848, the settlement's population exploded when gold was discovered in the surface soil of hilltops and gullies throughout the region. By 1854, more than 4,000 people lived in and around the settlement, consisting largely of the Chinese population from which it derives its name. In addition to cultural institutions, the Chinese laborers also brought gambling houses, opium dens, and their tongs.

Tongs were secret societies established for mutual support and protection, especially from other ethnic groups that were hostile to Chinese immigration. As tongs became better organized and stronger, they began claiming territories within a city or community and engaged in profitable, illegal activities that often brought them into conflict with each other. Many 19th century tongs operated in ways similar to the Italian-American Mafia of the 20th century. The Chinese operated gambling and prostitution houses, engaged in extortion, and smuggled people into the U.S. who were indentured as servants or prostitutes. From 1850 to 1920, several tong wars broke out in many American cities with large Chinese populations, including in San Francisco, Cleveland, and Los Angeles.

By 1855, members of four of the most powerful San Francisco tongs operated their clandestine activities in Chinese Camp. Small skirmishes were common, but on September 26, 1856, a large battle took place between 900 members of the Yan-Woo tong and 1,200 members of the Sam Yaps tong. Weapons were limited to pitch forks, rakes, and other farming and mining implements, so only four participants died although hundreds were wounded. This battle took place a few miles southwest of town, in the Red Hills at the junction of Red Hills Road and La Grange Road (J-59). People, including myself, who roam this site hoping to pick up paranormal hints of the Tong War have sensed strange environmental phenomena such as pockets of thickened atmosphere, the sensation of being pulled downward, or pressure against the skin as though being swatted by invisible beings. In addition to these sensations, I have found several places where the electromagnetic field intensifies, creating dizziness and nausea. Areas with intense EMF resemble lines. Stepping over the line creates transient sensations whereas standing on the line creates continuous symptoms. Intense EMF may mark the spots where tong warriors and miners faced off and died, exhibiting intense emotions such as fierce hostility or physical anguish.

In town, similar environmental remnants have been discovered in front of the post office, which opened on April 18, 1854. Ghosts roam along the façade of the building. As many as four apparitions of Chinese men have been sighted simultaneously as they leaned against the post office's iron shutters and brick wall. Some apparitions, dressed in prospector's clothing, have been seen as they hurry past the doorway. Often there is only a partial apparition, limited to part of a boot, an arm, or the head. EVP recorded at this location often yield the sound of heavy boots and indistinguishable words spoken in a guttural voice.

GHOSTS OF THE LITTLE CHURCH

St. Xavier Church
Main Street
Chinese Camp 95309

Erected in 1855, this little church high on a wooded knoll originally acted as an oasis of charity, mercy, and forgiveness amid a sea of greed, corruption, and crime. While the Chinese established Joss houses and other cultural centers, Anglo residents concerned themselves with building the tiny church that remains today as one of the few architectural remnants of the Gold Rush in this area.

Erected on a knoll at the edge of town, the church is surrounded by a cemetery that filled quickly with pioneers and miners, many of whom died at an early age from accidents, gunfights, or communicable diseases that swept through the camps. John Nicolini restored the church in 1949 and remains under the care of the Stockton archdiocese with maintenance funds provided by a local resident. No religious services have been held inside the church since 1928.

Ghostly sounds emanate from the church, audible to visitors in the cemetery. These sounds include a bell, organ music, voices raised in song, and the shuffling of heavy boots on the wood floor. I pressed my ear against the exterior wall and heard the organ and footsteps. I also heard the sound of a door swinging on rusty hinges, but no door was in motion at the time.

It is likely that intense environmental imprints from the 19th century remain in this building. The door locks and handles, floorboards, interior wood siding, and most of the pews are original. Intense, repetitive emotions generated by devoted parishioners during inspirational services, weddings, and funerals may be the basis of imprints that are sensed or triggered by psychics, sensitive ghost hunters, and others who can connect with the bygone era.

Throughout the cemetery sensitive people may feel odd sensations as though gravity has increased. Previously, I've described this as a sensation of heaviness, as if I had instantly gained 100 pounds. At the fenced gravesite to the left of the church the sensation of heaviness is strong. EVP at this site often reveal sobbing and a woman's voice uttering indistinct words as though she is trying to speak while crying.

THE TUCK-YOU-IN GHOST

Hotel Charlotte
18736 Main Street
Groveland 95321
209-962-6455
www.hotelcharlotte.com

If you check into this charming hotel and find yourself in room 6, you should expect to feel invisible hands tuck you into bed. The ghost that haunts that room is devoted to the hotel's guests and does all that she can to assure they are comfortable and cozy in bed. The hotel's owners and psychics who have investigated the place believe the nurturing ghost is that of the building's former owner, Charlotte DeFerrari.

Born in Genoa, Italy, in 1881, Charlotte immigrated to America at the age of 16, traveling with her mother, several siblings, and her father who hoped to get in on one of the lesser gold rushes that followed advances in mining technology and rising prices for gold. Dreams of striking it rich in California were short-lived, however. A few months after the family's arrival in Groveland, Charlotte's father was killed in a mining accident. Sixteen-year-old Charlotte became the family's sole breadwinner, working as a cook for local ranch hands and miners. Early in the 20th century, she opened her own restaurant in a building that now houses the town's popular Iron Door Saloon. This successful business generated the funds for construction of a fine hotel in 1918 and the addition of a restaurant in 1921. During construction of the Hetch Hetchy Dam and related water projects, workers boarded at the Hotel Charlotte and added to the prosperity of the DeFerrari family. When Charlotte died, she was mourned by hundreds and hailed as a local legend admired for her honesty, business skills, and gracious hospitality. With nearly lifelong devotion to the community and the hotel of her own design, it is no wonder the ghost of Charlotte DeFerrari cannot let go of the place and move on.

A psychic who visited the hotel captured the image of Charlotte's ghost in a photograph he took of a mirror hanging in room 6. There is no historical record that indicates why the ghost would be attached to this particular room, but local lore says Charlotte was in love with a man who visited the hotel often and always stayed in room 6. If this legend has some basis in fact, it might explain Charlotte's preoccupation with the comforts of male guests in this room.

THE FASTIDIOUS GHOST

Groveland Hotel
18767 Main Street
Groveland 95321
209-962-4000
www.groveland.com/

Some ghosts have behavioral quirks that provide ghost hunters with a reliable means of detecting their presence. These quirks include a fastidious nature to the extent that the ghost cannot tolerate any disturbance of the environment it haunts. The ghost may insist that closet doors are left open, books closed, drawers shut fully, lights turned on or off, magazines stacked neatly, or tables are kept clear of paraphernalia that belongs elsewhere. Spirits may become irritated with visitors who criticize the décor, furnishings, or odor of a place. Some may insist that beds are made, pillows aligned perfectly, or chairs pushed under a table. When this characteristic is discovered through research or interviews with witnesses, ghost hunters can create a successful investigation by causing the environmental disturbance that provokes the ghost to the greatest degree. The ghost that haunts room 15 of this historic hotel is easy to detect because he cannot tolerate women's cosmetics left on the dresser.

Lyle came to the Groveland Hotel in 1921. Most of what we know about Lyle comes from the oral history of local resident Ernie Greenbeck, who died in 1999 at the age of 104. According to Greenbeck, Lyle arrived long after the Gold Rush but made a very good living by panning in nearby creeks and contracting with other miners to perform blasting and other difficult and dangerous jobs. Lyle boarded in room 15 of the hotel for six years. It is reported that he purchased the dresser that is still used in his former room. When not working, Lyle dressed well but was known as a loner. He had few friends in town, so he wasn't missed until days after his death in 1927. His body was discovered in room 15, stretched out on the bed. The room was neat and clean, showing no signs of a bachelor's messiness. After the body was removed, the hotel's staff found Lyle's fancy clothes neatly folded and placed in the dresser. They also found a box of dynamite under the bed. Puzzled by this discovery, Greenbeck explained that Lyle used dynamite in his work as a prospector and miner.

Today Lyle haunts his old room and is as tidy as ever. Guests who stay in room 15 are often frustrated when they find that items left on the dresser are mysteriously removed. Women's cosmetics are often found in the sink or on the floor near the foot of the bed. Some astonished guests have actually witnessed cosmetics being moved by invisible hands. One woman watched her make-up case fly off the dresser. When reports are made to the hotel's manager, owner Peggy Mosley steps in and explains that the antics are due to the hotel's resident ghost, who is well liked and welcome to stay as long as he wishes.

Lyle also dislikes bright lights. Guests complain of lights that mysteriously dim while they are trying to read. Known as a prankster, Lyle has been blamed for missing items that turn up in odd places, strange light patterns on the hotel's computer screen, moving doors, and rearranged furniture. He seems to like candy, too. Sweets left in the room will be devoured, leaving only the telltale candy wrapper. Lyle's apparition has been seen by several staff members and guests. He appears as a dark figure, bearded with thinning hair. His clothing is not very defined, but the full-body apparition has been seen standing in the bathroom.

Ghost hunters who stay in room 15 should use women's cosmetics to arouse Lyle's interest and provoke paranormal activity. A video camera focused on the dresser top may capture Lyle removing those disagreeable items.

A HOST OF GHOSTS

Hotel Jeffery
1 Main Street
Coulterville 95311
209-878-3471
www.hoteljefferygold.com/

The historic Hotel Jeffery was constructed in 1851 on the remains of an adobe building that had been a Mexican fandango hall since 1849. First known as Banderita, meaning "little flag" in Spanish, the town was a wild and raucous mining camp that attracted a number of outlaws. Some of those bad guys were dispatched by mob justice that employed a hanging tree still standing across the street from Coulterville's park. In 1864, as the town's population had grown and civilized society exerted its influence over the rowdy miners and scavengers, the name was changed to honor George Wilson Coulter, whose businesses served as the core of what many thought would be the most important city in the Sierra foothills.

Much of the town was destroyed in the great flood of 1862 and again by fires in 1859, 1879, and 1899. The Hotel Jeffery suffered some damage in each of these disasters, but its foundation of stone and 30-inch-thick walls of adobe enabled owners to rebuild quickly and spearhead the resurgence of the community. After the original Mexican building was abandoned in 1851, George Jeffery acquired the property and gave his name to the hotel that still serves travelers today, including those who come to the foothills in search of gold or ghosts.

Several ghosts that date from the Gold Rush era have been detected in the Hotel Jeffery. In October of 2005, a respected organization called Central California Paranormal Investigators (CCPI) spent three days and nights in the hotel hunting the various spirits reported by guests and staff members. Equipped with EMF detectors, digital still cameras, film cameras, audio recorders, video cameras, a compass, and thermometers, CCPI concluded that two of their seven surveillance methodologies picked up clear evidence of paranormal activity. These two methodologies include still images of light phenomena and audio recordings of ten EVP. CCPI also discovered several locations within the hotel where a compass behaved erratically for no apparent reason and EMF anomalies occurred. These results were closely aligned with witness reports of ghostly activity in the saloon and dining room created by as many as 17 spirits.

In the hotel's Magnolia Saloon, the apparition of a miner has been spotted. He appears to be about 50 years old, with sunken eyes and dark, matted hair. This ghost may be responsible for draining the batteries of audio recorders used by ghost hunters. EMF fluctuations and orbs may also be attributable to this ghost. EVP recorded in the saloon include the voices of both men and women. Customers sitting alone in the saloon have reported the odor of cigar smoke and muted sound of lively conversations.

In the dining room, witnesses have reported seeing the ghost of a woman who worked in the hotel in the early 1900s. At times, she appears so lifelike that many people have reported details of her clothing, hair, and eyes. She is said to be about 30 and wears a long apron tied about her waist. This ghost rearranges place settings and overturns cups and plates on the tables after staff members have left for the night. She may be responsible for kitchen utensils that fly about and cold spots in both the dining room and kitchen.

Ghosts are also active in many of the guestrooms. In room 10, the apparition of a woman dressed in a long, white gown has been spotted walking across the room and sitting in the rocking chair. She stays for several minutes, rocking slowly, and then vanishes. In room 22, the ghosts of an older man and a younger woman appear with arms around each other. In room 3, a ghost child creates the sound of a ball rolling across the floor.

I stopped at the Hotel Jeffery three times over a span of two years. Each time, I spotted the torso and head of the ghostly miner in the Magnolia Saloon who sits at the far end of the bar on a stool. His thin hair looked brown and matted, as though it had not been washed in weeks. Soon after seeing this apparition, I detected the strong odor of stale whiskey and cigar smoke, yet no one was seated at the bar, and the bartender had not yet come on duty. On the stairs leading to the second floor, I saw the apparition of a maid who carried several towels in her arms.

Several other ghosts have been reported at various locations throughout the building. Several apparitions that include girls working as maids; a middle-aged, well-dressed woman; and a distinguished gentleman with a long moustache have been spotted in the hallways and many of the rooms. Ghost hunters who detect the odor of strong perfume should look nearby for the apparition of a woman in a red dress whose face is a chalky white.

LEGAL GHOSTS

Mariposa Courthouse
5088 Bullion Street
Mariposa 95338
209-966-2005

A bizarre event straight from the pages of Larry McMurtry's *Lonesome Dove* created one of the ghosts that haunt the historic Mariposa County Courthouse. After a quick trial that ended with a death sentence for murderer, Tom Peck, the condemned man, stood on the second floor of the courthouse listening to the angry mob gathering in the street below. As shouts of "Lynch him!" filled the courthouse grounds and echoed through the building, Peck opted for the easy way out, robbing the vigilantes of the satisfaction of hanging him. Breaking away from the deputy, Peck jumped through a second-floor window and killed himself on the rock-hard ground below.

Legend says the deputy, in trying to restrain Peck, followed him through the window and also died, although I could find no corroboration for that part of the story. Ghost hunters who have seen the TV mini-series *Lonesome Dove* may recall this same event as the outlaw Blue Duck escaped hanging by jumping through a window to his death.

Spirit remnants, or environmental imprints, can still be found on both floors of this historic building. Constructed in 1854 of white pine, carpenters hand-planed every plank and used no nails in joining the supporting structure. These skilled craftsmen also created the benches that have been used in the courthouse for more than 150 years. Marks from their planes and signs of wear from the backsides of lawyers, criminals, and spectators are easy to find. Also evident are isolated cold spots at several locations on many of the benches, the sound of a gavel when court is not in session, and light anomalies caught on film and in digital images.

The apparitions of several men dressed in 19th-century suits have been spotted near the pot-bellied stove. When these spirits aren't visible, sensitive ghost hunters can hear the low murmur of their hushed conversations. A colleague of mine who is a gifted psychic discovered emotional remnants of what could be Tom Peck's suicidal leap near a window on the west wall. After this location was pointed out to me, I could detect a bizarre rush of thickened air moving horizontally toward the closed window.

GUNFIGHTING GHOSTS

Hornitos Road from State Highway 140
Hornitos 95306
www.ghosttowns.com/states/ca/hornitos.html

Hornitos is remote, strangely quiet, and most of the structures date from the mid-1800s, lending it such an authentic feeling of being occupied by ghosts that one might mistake the residents as such. Travelers heading to Yosemite National Park or the southern Gold Rush country from central and southern California pass close by this fascinating village, but most do not take the turn-off or the time to explore a truly amazing haunted town. The desolate graveyard, crumbling wooden houses, weathered brick buildings, and small streets are full of ghostly apparitions and other paranormal phenomena, including unexplained odors, sounds, light anomalies, cold spots, and creepy feelings of being watched by a being standing close behind you.

Hornitos was established by Mexican ranchers before the Gold Rush. With the invasion of 300,000 gold seekers, the town prospered by selling beef and other farm products. Quick wealth brought gambling and fandango halls, bars, brothels, and other unsavory businesses, which attracted many undesirable characters who had been run out of larger towns. Some outlaws, such as the notorious Joaquin Murrieta, sought refuge among the Mexican population in Hornitos where they would blend in and, perhaps, go unrecognized, soon overwhelming the little town with their debauchery and violence. Law and order were restored when some of the town's founders prevailed upon the governor to drive out or capture criminals and close many of the dens of vice.

By 1859, Hornitos was attracting law-abiding citizens who opened legitimate businesses, including the Ghirardelli chocolate factory and a Wells Fargo office, and built a school and the St. Catherine Catholic Church. Today, many of these buildings are ruins, giving Hornitos the appearance of a real ghost town.

St. Catherine's cemetery is filled with headstones that have been damaged by wind, weather, and the passage of time. At night, the place is truly spooky, but overcoming their fear is worthwhile for ghost hunters when they find orbs and other light anomalies in nearly all their photographs. At the fallen headstone of William and Mary McCullough, both of whom died in infancy, I've spotted the apparition of a child. The ghost I saw appeared to be about eight years old. This may be the ghost of an older sibling looking after the grave of his baby brother and sister.

The Wells Fargo building harbors many noisy ghosts. Standing at the doors of this building, people can hear boots treading the wood floor that is no longer there, bells ringing, and heavy doors opening and closing.

At many of the crumbling wooden houses, strange lights are often seen. Ghost hunters should not enter these structures because they are unsafe, but looking through windows and doors may reveal the ghosts of former residents.

The best time to visit Hornitos is at twilight, but I recommend you arrive during daylight hours and get acquainted with the town before nightfall. Visit the graveyard and a few buildings that appeal to your senses and devise a plan for safely observing ghosts after sunset. Keep in mind that many of the haunted buildings in this town are structurally unsafe.

Other places to hunt ghosts:

THE OLD STONE JAIL

Bullion Street, between 5th and 4th Streets
Mariposa 95338
209-966-2924
www.visitmariposa.net/jailtour.htm

Built in 1858 from locally quarried granite, this jail was used to incarcerate drunks, claim jumpers, thieves, con men, and murderers. The place was so busy with capital offenders that a gallows was erected at the east end of building. In spite of the building's sturdy appearance, several successful escape attempts were orchestrated by inmates who banded together to overpower the guards. In 1892, Thomas Truitt tried to escape his cell by setting his straw mattress on fire. Truitt escaped the hard way, as a spirit, leaving behind his charred body. Today, his ghost, or that one of the many men who were executed on the gallows, haunts this jail.

THE OLD MASONIC HALL

4994 6th Street
Mariposa 95338
209-966-1333

Built in 1917 as a meeting hall and social center for local Masons, the tall, white building now houses the Sixth Street Cinema. Strange things happen on both floors, but the most active spirit seems to prefer the cinema that operates on the second floor. The transparent apparition of a tall, thin gentleman appears in all areas of the second floor, as if he is watching over it. When I saw him, he was wearing a dark, cut-away coat. His white shirt was nearly covered by a long beard. Across his lap was a white garment that looked like a small apron and may be the ceremonial apron worn by Masons.

THE PUBLIC CEMETERY

Cemetery Street
Coulterville 95311

This pioneer cemetery is only a short distance from well-traveled Highway 49 and well worth the time it takes for a visit, especially at twilight. Most of Coulterville's early developers are buried here, including George Jeffery, builder of the Hotel Jeffery, and George Wilson Coulter, the town's namesake. Many believe Coulter's spirit loiters near his grave. An unidentified dark figure also roams this graveyard, showing up most often near the gate as if he is waiting for someone in particular. This spirit appears to be wearing a hooded cape that hides his face.

WHISTLING WILLIE AND THE HANGING TREE

Highway 49 (across the street from the town park)
Coulterville 95311

The historic steam engine "Whistling Willie" sits under the hangman's tree as a monument to the railroad that carried tons of gold ore from the Mary Harrison Mine to the Black Creek Potosi Mill, where the gold was extracted and stamped. Some surprised visitors have heard sounds the engine would make if it were operational. These include the sounds of hissing steam and grinding wheels.

Whistling Willie sits under the hangman's tree that was used to administer justice in Coulterville. In 1856, Leon Ruiz was hanged from this tree for robbing and murdering two Chinese miners. It is said that the apparitions of men hanging from the branches can occasionally be seen.

Sighting Report Form

GENERAL INSTRUCTIONS

Photocopy and enlarge the form on the next page to a standard 8.5 x 11 inch format.

This form should be completed immediately after a sighting. If the ghost hunt is performed by a group, a designated leader should assume the role of reporter. The reporter is responsible for completing this form.

The reporter and each witness should make a statement, either audio or written, describing in full their experience at the site. Date, sign, and label these statements with a reference number identical to the report number on the sighting report form. Attach the statements to the report form.

SIGHTING REPORT

SITE NAME _____ REPORT # _____
LOCATION _____ DATE: _____
_____ TIME:_____
REPORTER _____ SITE # _____
WITNESSES _____
_____
_____

DESCRIPTION OF APPARITION _____

_____

temperature change   [ ] YES   [ ] NO
auditory phenomena   [ ] YES   [ ] NO
telekinesis   [ ] YES   [ ] NO
visual phenomena   [ ] YES   [ ] NO
other phenomena   [ ] YES   [ ] NO
Description:

Use the reverse side for diagrams, maps, and drawings.
SPECIFIC LOCATION WITHIN SITE: _____

_____

PREVIOUS SIGHTINGS AT THIS SITE?: [ ] YES [ ] NO
Reference:_____
Summary:_____

RECORDS:
audio   [ ] YES   [ ] NO   Ref. No. _____
video   [ ] YES   [ ] NO   Ref. No. _____
photo   [ ] YES   [ ] NO   Ref. No. _____
Summary of Records: _____
Disposition of records: _____

_____

WITNESS STATEMENTS - Summary: _____

_____

audio   [ ] YES   [ ] NO
written [ ] YES   [ ] NO

Disposition of statements: _____

_____

Suggested Reading

BOOKS

Allison, Ross and Joe Teeples. *Ghostology 101: Becoming a Ghost Hunter.* Authorhouse, 2005.

Auerbach, Lloyd. *ESP, Hauntings, and Poltergeists.* New York: Warner Books, New York 1986.

———. *Ghost Hunting: How to Investigate the Paranormal.* Oakland, CA: Ronin Publishing, 2004.

Bardens, Dennis. *Ghosts and Hauntings.* Lincoln, NE: IUniverse 2000.

Belanger, Jeff. *The World's Most Haunted Places.* Franklin Lakes, NJ: Career Press, 2004.

Bradley, Nancy. *The Incredible World of Gold Rush Ghosts: True Tales of Hauntings in the Mother Lode.* Kearney, NE: Morris Publishing, 1998.

Bradley, Nancy and Vincent Gaddis. *Gold Rush Ghosts.* Garberville, CA: Borderland Sciences Research Foundation, 1990.

Browne, Sylvia. *Adventures of a Psychic.* New York: Penguin Books, 1990.

Cornell, Tony. *Investigating the Paranormal.* New York: Helix Press, 2002.

Dwyer, Jeff. *Ghost Hunter's Guide to the Bay Area.* Gretna, LA: Pelican Publishing, 2005.

———. *Ghost Hunter's Guide to Los Angeles.* Gretna, LA: Pelican Publishing, 2007.

———. *Ghost Hunter's Guide to New Orleans.* Gretna, LA: Pelican Publishing, 2007.

———. *Ghost Hunter's Guide to Seattle.* Gretna, LA: Pelican Publishing, 2008.

Garcez, Antonio. *Ghost Stories of California's Gold Rush Country and Yosemite National Park.* Placitas, NM: Red Rabbit Press, 2004.

Hauck, Dennis William. *Haunted Places: The National Directory.* New York: Penguin Group, 2002.

Holzer, Hans. *Ghosts: True Encounters with the World Beyond.* New York: Black Dog and Leventhal Publishers, 2004.

————. *Ghosts I've Met.* New York: Barnes and Noble Books, 2005.

————. *Hans Holzer's Travel Guide to Haunted Houses.* New York: Black Dog and Leventhral Publishers, Inc. 1998.

————. *True Ghost Stories.* New York: Barnes and Noble Books, 2001.

Lankford, Andrea. *Haunted Hikes: Spine-tingling Tales and Trails from North America's National Park System.* Santa Monica Press, 2006.

Martinez, Raymond. *Marie Laveau, Voodoo Queen.* Gretna, LA: Pelican Publishing , 2001.

Mead, Robin. *Haunted Hotels: A Guide to American and Canadian Inns and Their Ghosts.* Nashville, TN: Rutledge Hill Press, 1995.

Miller, Richard. *Ghost Towns of California: Remnants of the Mining Digs.* Arizona: Renaissance House Publishers, 1992.

Ramsland, Katherine. *Ghost: Investigating the Other Side.* New York: St. Martin's Press, 2001.

Reinstedt, Randall. *California Ghost Notes.* Carmel, CA: Ghost Town Publications, 2000.

Rule, Leslie. *Coast to Coast Ghosts: True Stories of Hauntings Across America.* Kansas City, MO: Andrews McMeel Publishing, 2001.

Smith, Barbara. *Ghost Stories of California.* Renton, WA: Lone Pin Publishing, 2000.

Southall, R.H. *How to be a Ghost Hunter.* St. Paul, MN: Llewellyn Publications, 2003.

Steiger, Brad. *Real Ghosts, Restless Spirits, and Haunted Places.* Detroit: Visible Ink Press, 2003

Taylor, Troy. *Ghost Hunter's Guidebook.* Alton, IL: Whitechapel Productions Press, 1999.

Varney, Philip. *Ghost Towns of Northern California.* Osceola, WI: Voyageur Press, 2001.

Warner, Joshua. *How to Hunt for Ghosts: A Practical Guide.* New York: Fireside Press, 2003.

Watson, James. *Big Bad Bodie: High Sierra Ghost Town.* Bandon, OR: Robert D. Reed Publishers, 2002.

Winer, Richard. *Ghost Ship: True Stories of Nautical Nightmares, Hauntings and Disasters.* New York: Berkeley Publishing Group, 2000.

Wlodarski, Robert and Anne Wlodarski. *California Hauntaspitality.* Alton, IL: White Chapel Productions Press, 2002.

ARTICLES

Auerback, Lloyd. "Lloyd Auerback Shares Tales from the Dark Side." *San Francisco Chronicle,* October 30, 1998.

Barrett, Greg. "Can the living talk to the dead? Psychics say they connect with the other world, but skeptics respond: 'Prove it.'" *USA Today,* June 20, 2001.

Berkeley, Sarah. "Haunted Sonoma." *Sonoma,* Fall 2007.

Burkin, Christian. "Group of ghost hunters scours signs." *Stockton Record,* April 15, 2007.

Cadden, Mary. "Get spooked on a walking tour." *USA Today,* October 17, 2003.

Calvan, Bobby Caina. "Ghost of a chance. *Sacramento Bee,* January 22, 2008.

Clark, Jayne. "10 great places to get spooked by your surroundings." *USA Today,* October 26, 2007.

Evans, Will. "Is Sacramento a ghost town?" *Sacramento Bee,* October 31, 2002.

Finnegan, Lora. "Secrets of Bodie—California Ghost Town." *Sunset,* July 2000.

Fullwood, Janet. "Ghost town of Bodie resurrects a long-lost West." *Sacramento Bee,* October 4, 2006.

Giovannetti, Joe. "Crossing over: Ghost hunter knows things that go bump in the night." *Fairfield (CA) Daily Republic,* October 18, 2007.

Hill, Angela. "Paranormal experts say it's not all funny. *Oakland (CA) Tribune,* October 18, 2002.

Kelly, Leslie. "On dining: Hungry for a good scare? Try these haunts." *Seattle Post-Intelligencer,* October 30, 2007.

Kim, Gina. "Grave Tales." *Sacramento Bee,* October 31, 2006.

Lee, Luaine. "Tuolumne County: Tourist gold in these California hills." *Orange County Register,* November 4, 2007.

Massingill, T. "Business of ghost busting." *Contra Costa Times,* October 8, 2000.

May, Antoinette. "Rooms and a 'Boo.'" *Stockton (CA) Record,* October 26, 2003.

Moller, Dave. "Ghost searchers to probe U.S. Hotel." *The Union,* June 23, 2007.

Moran, Gwen. "Real-Life Ghost Busters." *USA Weekend,* October 31, 2004.

Nowacki, Kim. "Here's how real ghost-hunters work." *Yakima Herald-Republic,* October 20, 2003.

Philips, Jeff. "Coloma, about those ghosts—you're kidding, right?" *Sunset,* October 1992.

Schoolmeester, Ron. "10 great places to go on a haunted hike." *USA Today,* July 28, 2006.

Sichelman, Lew. "Plenty of spooky sites around the nation." *San Francisco (CA) Chronicle,* October 28, 2007.

Trump, Jamie. "Folsom's haunted history." *Folsom (CA) Telegraph,* October 25, 2005.

Organizations

You may contact these organizations to report ghost phenomena, obtain advice, or arrange for an investigation of a haunting. Many of these organizations conduct conferences, offer training, or list educational opportunities for those seeking to become paranormal investigators.

Amateur Ghost Hunters of Seattle/Tacoma (AGHOST)
253-203-4383
E-mail: aghost@aghost.us
Web site: www.aghost.us/index.html

American Society for Psychical Research
5 West 73rd Street
New York, NY 10023
212-799-5050

Berkeley Psychic Institute
2436 Hastings Street
Berkeley, CA 94704
510-548-8020

British Society for Psychical Research
Eleanor O'Keffe, secretary
49 Marloes Road
London W86LA
+44-71-937-8984

Committee for Scientific Investigations of Claims of the Paranormal
1203 Kensington Avenue
Buffalo, NY 14215

Department of Psychology
Jordan Hall, Building 420
Stanford University
Stanford, CA 94305

Division of Parapsychology
Box 152, Medical Center
Charlottesville, VA 22908

Ghost Hunters of the South (GHOTS)
Web site: www.ghots.net

Ghost Trackers
P.O. Box 89
Santa Clara, CA 95052
408-244-8331
E-mail: ghosttrackers@yahoo.com
Web site: www.ghost-trackers.org

Haunted and Paranormal Investigations
Web site: www.therealghosthunters.com

Institute for Parapsychology
Box 6847
College Station
Durham, NC 27708

International Society for Paranormal Research
4712 Admiralty Way
Marina del Rey, CA 90292

International Ghost Hunter's Organization
Web site: www.ghostweb.com/ondex.html

Louisiana Paranormal Research Society
725 Misty Lane
Lake Charles, LA 70611
Web site: www.louisianaparanormal.com

Office of Paranormal Investigations
JFK University
12 Altarinda Road
Orinda, CA 94563
415-249-9275

Orange County Paranormal Research Group
E-mail: OCPR@OCPRgroup.com
Web site: www.ocprgroup.com

San Diego Paranormal Research Project
E-mail: Info@SDparanormal.com
Web site: www.SDparanormal.com

Southern California Society for Psychical Research
269 South Arden Boulevard
Los Angeles, CA 90004

Washington State Ghost Society
Website: www.washingtonstateghostsociety.org/

Films, DVDs, and Videos

Fictional films may provide you with information that will assist you in preparing for a ghost hunt. This assistance ranges from putting you in the proper mood for ghost hunting to useful techniques for exploring haunted places. Some films, especially documentaries may provide information about the nature of ghostly activity.

America's Most Haunted Town (2001). Documentary. Directed by Robert Child.

America's Most Haunted Inns (2004). Documentary. Directed by Robert Child.

Beyond Belief: Investigation into the Paranormal (2006). Documentary.

Carrie (1976). Directed by Brian De Palma. Starring Sissy Spacek and Piper Laurie.

Cemetery Man (1994). Directed by Michele Soavi. Starring Rupert Everett and Francois Hadji-Lazaro.

Changeling (1980). Directed by Peter Medak. Starring George C. Scott and Trish VanDevere

City of Angels (1998). Directed by Brad Silberling. Starring Nicolas Cage and Meg Ryan.

Dragonfly (2002). Starring Kevin Costner and Kathy Bates.

The Entity (1983). Directed by Sidney J. Furie. Starring Barbara Hershey, Ron Silver.

Frighteners (1996). Directed by Peter Jackson. Starring Michael J. Fox and Trini Alvarado.

Ghost Machine (2009). Directed by Chris Hartwill. Starring Sean Faris and Rachael Taylor.

Ghost of Flight 409 (1987). Made for TV. Directed by Steven Hilliard Stern. Starring Ernest Borgnine and Kim Bassinger.

Ghosts of England and Belgrave Hall (2001). Documentary.

Ghost Ship (2002). Directed by Steve Beck. Starring Julianna Margulies and Ron Eldard.

Ghost Story (1981). Directed by John Irvin. Starring Fred Astaire and Melvyn Douglas.

Ghost Stories, Volume 1 (1997). Documentary hosted by Patrick McNee.

Ghost Stories, Volume 2 (1997). Documentary hosted by Patrick McNee.

Haunted (1995). Directed by Lewis Gilbert. Starring Aidan Quinn and Kate Beckinsale.

Haunted History. History Channel Home Video. Documentary.

Haunted History of Halloween. History Channel Home Video. Documentary.

Haunted Houses. A & E Home Video. Documentary.

Haunted Places (2001). Documentary by Christopher Lewis.

Haunting (1999). Directed by Jan De Bont. Starring Liam Neeson and Catherine-Zeta Jones.

Haunting Across America (2001). Documentary hosted by Michael Dorn.

Haunting of Seacliff Inn (1995). Directed by Walter Klenhard. Starring Ally Sheedy and William R. Moses.

Hollywood Ghosts and Gravesites (2003). Documentary.

Living With the Dead (2000). Directed by Stephen Gyllenhaal. Starring Ted Danson and Mary Steenburgen.

Mysterious Forces Beyond: Vol. 2: Death and Paranormal (2002). Documentary.

The Others (2001). Directed by Alejandro Amenabar. Starring Nicole Kidman and Christopher Eccleston.

Poltergeist (1982). Directed by Tobe Hooper. Starring JoBeth Williams and Craig T. Nelson.

Poltergeist II: The Other Side (1986). Directed by Brian Gibson. Starring JoBeth Williams and Craig T. Nelson.

Restless Spirits (1999). Directed by David Wellington. Starring Lothaire Bluteau, Michel Monty, and Marsha Mason.

Sightings: Heartland Ghost (2002). Directed by Brian Trenchard-Smith. Starring Randy Birch and Beau Bridges.

Shutter (2008). Directed by Masayuki Ochiai. Starring Joshua Jackson and Rachael Taylor.

The Sixth Sense (1999). Directed by M. Night Shyamalan. Starring Bruce Willis and Haley Joel Osment.

White Noise (2005). Directed by Geoffrey Sax. Starring Michael Keaton.

13 Ghosts (2001). Directed by Steve Beck. Starring Tony Shalhoub.

1408 (2007). Directed by Mikael Hafstrom. Starring John Cusack and Samuel L. Jackson.

The following movies are not about ghosts, but they are worth watching before visiting California's Gold Rush country. They provide a sneak preview of some of the scenery and a bit of local culture. Go to www.columbiagazette.com/films.html for a partial list of the 300 movies filmed in Tuolumne County.

High Noon (1952). Directed by Fred Zinnemann. Starring Gary Cooper and Lloyd Bridges. Several scenes were filmed on Columbia's main street.

Three Bad Men (2004). Directed by Jeff Hathcock. Starring Chris Gann and George Kennedy. Several locations in Columbia were used, including the St. Charles Saloon, in front of the D. H. Mills Bank, and near the Columbia Gazette office.

Back to the Future, Part III (1990). Directed by Robert Zemeckis. Starring Michael J. Fox and Christopher Lloyd. A complete town was fabricated near Jamestown and used as a movie set. The chase scenes will give you a great view of the Sierra foothills country.

Pale Rider (1985). Directed by Clint Eastwood. Starring Clint Eastwood and John Russell. The movie depicts hydraulic mining as it was practiced around Placerville. When Clint rides into town, he travels on horseback down Columbia's main street and then enters the Wells Fargo building to retrieve his guns. A good view is offered of the interior of this building.

Internet Resources

www.jeffdwyer.com. Web site of paranormal investigator, ghost hunter, and writer Jeff Dwyer.

www.goldrushghosts.com. Gold Rush Ghosts is an organization dedicated to the investigation of haunted places with am emphasis on debunking claims reports of paranormal events.

www.hpiparanormal.net. Haunted and Paranormal Investigations is a highly active group of ghost hunters who have considerable experience with Sacramento-area and Gold Rush country spirits. E-mail: ghost@ snmproductionsco.com

www.ghost-trackers.org. Ghost Trackers are a professional research group based in the San Francisco Bay Area. Among their members are scientists and experts technicians. E-mail: ghostttrackers@yahoo.com

www.therealghosthunters.com. The San Joaquin Valley Paranormal Investigators cover the Central Valley and parts of Northern California.

www.aa-evp.com. The American Association for Electronic Voice Phenomena, founded by Sarah Estep, offers advice, and opportunities to learn new EVCP techniques.

www.californiahistoricalsociety.org. This is the official site of the California Historical Society, offering publications and several links that can help ghost hunter research specific events, historical figures, or historic sites.

www.californiahistory.com. This site offers several articles about California history that serve as useful orientation for visitors from distant parts of the U.S. E-mail: cahist@aol.com

www.prarieghosts.com/ghost_hunt.html. This is the official Web site of the American Ghost Society, founded by authors and ghost researchers Troy and Amy Taylor. This site provides information about ghost research, paranormal investigations, and books written by Troy Taylor.

www.the-atlantic-paranormal-society.com. This organization has more than 50 groups throughout the U.S. that have demonstrated excellence and discretion in their investigations of the paranormal.

www.ispr.net/home.html. The International Society for Paranormal Research, headed by Dr. Larry Montz, conducts ghost expeditions, provides the media with expert opinions on paranormal issues, and lists classes and products of interest to ghost hunters.

www.ghoststore.net. This Web site catalogues a vast array of ghost hunting equipment available for purchase.

www.paranormality.com/ghost_hunting_equipment.shtml. The Web site displays high-tech equipment useful in paranormal investigations.

www.ghostresearch.org. The Ghost Research Society was established in 1971 as a investigative body specializing in reports of paranormal activity. Members research homes and businesses and analyze photographs and audio and video recordings to establish authenticity. The organization is headed by well-known ghost researcher Dale Kaczmarek.

www.ghostweb.com. The International Ghost Hunters Society, headed by Drs. Sharon Gill and Dave Oester, researches spirits to produce evidence of life after death. The society also offers a home-study certification for paranormal investigators. Membership exceeds 15,000.

www.nationalghosthunters.com/investigations.html. This is the official

Web site of the National Ghost Hunters Society. This organization of psychics and mediums helps people solve problems they have with ghosts.

www.ghosthunter.com. This is the Web site of ghost hunter and lecturer Patti Starr.

www.marylandghosts.com. The Maryland Ghost and Spirit Association, founded by Beverly Litsinger, investigates Civil War sites in Maryland, Virginia, Pennsylvania, and other haunted locations.

www.mindreader.com. The Office of Paranormal Investigations, directed by internationally renowned author and researcher Lloyd Auerbach, investigates a variety of paranormal activity for a fee. Information about current and former investigations is available to serious researchers and the media.

www.ghost-stalker.com. Richard Senate, well-known author, lecturer, and ghost investigator, focuses mainly on Southern California locations.

www.washingtonstateghostsociety.org. Washington State Ghost Society is a non-profit organization that assists individuals who have experienced paranormal phenomena.

www.theshadowlands.net/ghost. This is a directory of reports of unsubstantiated hauntings and other paranormal events organized by state. This is a good Web site for finding places that might be hot spots for ghostly activity.

www.historichotels.nationaltrust.org. Historic hotels of America are detailed here.

www.paranormal.com. This Web site has a live chat room and links to news articles about paranormal activities.

www.ghosttowns.com. This informative Web site gives detailed information about ghost towns in the U.S. and Canada.

www.psi-app.com. PSI is a north California organization dedicated to the investigation and documentation of anomalous events, including the paranormal.

www.the-atlantic-paranormal-society.com. This is the official Web site of the Atlantic Paranormal Society (TAPS). This group of ghost investigators gained famed through the SciFi Channel program *Ghost Hunter.*

www.ghostresearch.com. This is a Web site for information about ghost hunting methods, equipment, and on-going investigations.

www.nps.gov. Here the National Park Service lists several hundred historic sites.

www.ghots.net. This is the Web site for Ghost Hunters of the South, an association of researchers and investigators.

www.aghost.us/index.html. Amateur Ghost Hunters of Seattle-Tacoma is a well-organized, highly active group of researchers, investigators, and consultants. AGHOST has been featured on several television programs. The group stages the annual Pacific Northwest Ghost Hunter's Conference each fall.

www.hollowhill.com. This is a ghost information Web site that displays reports, photographs, eyewitness reports, location information, and ghost hunting techniques.

www.scghs.com. The Southern California Ghost Hunters Society performs investigations of haunted locations and provides consultations.

Special Tours and Events

Columbia Tour: This 52-minute walking tour takes you throughout the streets of an authentic 1850s Gold Rush town. The town has been beautifully preserved, giving visitors a rare view of bars, banks, a Wells Fargo office, a blacksmith's barn, and inns. $8.00. 209-532-0150. www.columbiacalifornia.com

Placerville Tour: Every Saturday morning, rain or shine, this one-hour tour takes visitors to many historic places in old Auburn. Meet the tour guide at the old Courthouse at 101 Maple Street. Free. 530-889-6500.

Old Sacramento Ghost Tour: This tour is offered only on weekends in October. One-hour tours, led by costumed docents, start at the Living History Center (1101 Second Street) at 6:30, 7:00, 7:30, and 8:00 P.M. Adults $15.00, children $12.00. Reservations required. 916-445-3101. www.oldsacramentolivinghistory.com/

Old Sacramento City Cemetery Tours: The cemetery committee offers tours on Friday the 13th and weekends in October in recognition of Halloween. Call 916-264-5621 or go to www.oldcitycemetery.com for information and reservations.

Kennedy Mine Tour: Visible from the historic Highway 49, the Kennedy Mine is located one mile north of Jackson. The mine's foundation offers guided and self-guide surface tours of the historic gold mine. This 90-minute tour is a great way to learn about the hard life miners faced, the wealth they produced, and the dangers that sometimes took their lives. Adults $9.00, children $5.00. 209-223-9542. www.kennedygoldmine.com

Empire Mine State Historic Park: For more than 100 years, the Empire Mine was one of the largest, deepest, longest-operating, and richest hard rock gold mines in the world, producing more than six million ounces of gold. Located in Grass Valley, the park offers tours that include the owner's home. The mine is located at 10791 East Empire Street in Grass Valley. 530-273-8522. www.parks.ca.gov

Gabby's Historic Gold Rush Tours: This company offers several guided tours that will provide ghost hunters with an excellent orientation to the region and the historic Gold Rush. The Immigrant Trail tour takes visitors on an all-day trek to Carson Pass for a walk on ground tread by thousands of pioneers as they crossed the Sierras in the early 1850s. This tour is 8 hours and $110.00 per person. The Gold Discovery tour includes visits to several historic sites near Placerville and locations along the American River. An underground tour of the Gold Bug Mine is also on the agenda. All day; $110 person. 209-296-3106. www.gabbysgoldrushtours.com. E-mail: gabby@gabbysgoldrushtours.com

Bodie State Historic Park: This famous Gold Rush ghost town is high on the list of must-sees for serious ghost hunters. The town consists of more than 150 structures that remain in a state of arrested decay. Self-guided tours are offered year round. Docent-led tours are available only in the summer. Bodie is about 20 miles from Bridgeport on the eastern side of the Sierra Nevada. Its remote location makes passage subject to weather conditions. 760-647-6445. www.parks.ca./gov. E-mail: bodie@qnet.com.

Ghosts of Bridgeport Tour: This special tour is offered only once a year, on the weekend before Halloween. Knowledgeable docents will lead you to some of the most fascinating places in this remote town. Given its remote location, ghost hunters might want to combine this event with a visit to Bodie and be careful of weather threats. 960-432-2546.

Nevada City Ghost Tour: Local story-teller Mark Lyon offers a tour of the Gold Rush town's most fascinating haunted sites. Destinations include the Doris Foley Library, Nevada Theatre, and Firehouse No. 1 on Main Street. Offered Saturday evenings, late June through October. Adults $10.00, children $5.00. 530-265-6877.

Mercer Caverns Tours: This spectacular cave in Murphys was used by prehistoric Indians as a mortuary. Bodies were dropped into the cave and allowed to roll to its depths where they were left. Tours began in 1885 and continue to amaze visitors who are hearty enough to venture deep underground. Forty-five-minute guided tours offer ghost hunters opportunities for photography and EVP recording. Adults $12.00, children $7.00. 209-728-2101. www.mercercaverns.com/html/tours.html

Moaning Cavern Tour: Rappel down a 165-foot-long rope into this amazing cave. The tour takes you to the spot where bones of prehistoric Indians have been discovered. You will learn how the moaning cavern got its name. The cave is located in Vallecito, between the towns of Murphys and Angels Camp, at 53250 Moaning Cave Road. Adults $12.95, children $6.50. 866-762-2837. www.cavetoursd.com/moaningdir.html

Historical Societies and Museums

Historical societies and museums are good places to discover information about old houses and other buildings or places that figure prominently in local history. They often contain records in the form of old newspapers, diaries, and photographs about calamitous events such as fires, hangings, train wrecks, and earthquakes that led to the loss of life. Old photographs and maps may be available to serious researchers that are not on display for public viewing.

Alpine County Museum
1 School Street
Markleeville 96120
530-694-2317

Amador Whitney Museum
14170 Old Amador Road
Sutter Creek 95685
209-267-0928

Angels Camp City Museum
753 S. Main Street
Angeles Camp 95222
209-736-2963

Calaveras County Museum and Archives
46 Main Street
Valley Springs 95252
209-754-3918

California State Mining Museum
5005 Fairgrounds Road
Mariposa 95338
209-742-7625
Web site: www.minerals.state.nv.us

Coarse Gold Historical Society
31889 Highway 41
Coarsegold 93614
559-642-4448

Discovery Museum Gold Rush History Center
915 I Street
Sacramento 95814
916-264-7211

El Dorado County Historical Museum
104 Placerville Drive
Placerville 95667
Web site: www.co.eldorado.ca.us/museum

El Dorado County Historical Society
524 Main Street
Placerville 95667
530-626-0773

Emigrant Trail Museum (Commemorating the Donner party)
12593 Donner Pass Road
Truckee 96161
530-582-7892

Folsom History Museum
823 Sutter Street
Folsom 95630
916-985-2707
Web site: www.folsomhistorymuseum.org
E-mail: info@folsomhistorymuseum.org

Forest Hill Divide Museum
24601 Harrison Street
Foresthill 95631
530-367-3988

Fountain and Tall Museum
524 Main Street
Placerville 95667
530-626-0773

Gold Country Museum
1273 High Street
Auburn 95603
530-887-0690

Grass Valley Museum
410 South Church Street
Grass Valley 95945
530-273-5509
Web site: www.saintjosephculturalcenter.org

Joss House Museum
200 Sacramento Street
Auburn 95603
530-823-0373

Lake Tahoe Historic Society Museum
3058 Highway 50
Lake Tahoe 96145
530-541-5458

Mariposa Museum and History Center
5119 Jessie Street
Mariposa 95338
209-966-2924

Mono Basin Historical Society
129 Mattley Avenue
Lee Vining 93541
760-647-6461

Mono County Museum
129 Emigrant Street
Bridgeport 93517
760-932-5281

Nevada County Historical Society
Allison Ranch Road at McCourtney
Grass Valley 95945
530-273-4255

Nevada County Historical Society
Firehouse Museum
214 Main Street
Nevada City 95959
530-265-2044

Placer County Archives
11437 D Avenue
Auburn 95603
530-889-7789

Placer County Museums
7504 Rock Springs Road
Penryn 95663
916-663-1837

Roseville Historical Society
557 Lincoln Street
Roseville 95678

Tuolumne City Memorial Museum
18663 Carter Street
Tuolumne 95379
209-928-3516

Tuolumne County Museum and History Center
158 West Bradford Avenue
Sonora 95370
209-532-1317

Underground Gold Miners Museum
356 Main Street
Alleghany 95910
530-287-3330
Web site: www.ncgold.com

Wells Fargo History Museum
1000 2nd Street
Sacramento 95814
916-440-4263
Web site: www.wellsfargohistory.com

Yuba City Historical Society
330 9th Street
Marysville 95

Index